The Equality Act for Educatic Professionals

Under the Equality Act (2010), all schools and service providers have a legal obligation to make provision for pupils, staff and school users with disabilities. If you're feeling confused and concerned about the content and implications of the Disability Discrimination Act (1995) and the more recent Equality Act (2010), and how it affects your setting, this essential book will help you unpick the issues in a user-friendly and easily accessible way.

This highly practical resource:

- explains the main parts of the Equality Act (2010) as it affects disability in a way that will encourage all members of staff within a school to feel confident that they are correctly implementing its requirements;
- discusses 'reasonable adjustments', and 'less favourable treatment', which are at the heart of the legislation;
- shows how less favourable treatment and reasonable adjustments apply to admissions, exclusions, handling of medicines and during school trips;
- uses examples and case studies throughout, and highlights the key factors for success in making reasonable adjustments;
- takes readers through the process of an alleged act of discrimination against the school, and how it may be resolved, up to and including the SEND tribunal process.

The author brings a wealth of experience to this topic, both as a parent of a child with disabilities and as a trainer of professionals. She uses her unique insight to develop skills and awareness in anyone who follows her material, and shows, through tried-and-tested concepts and methods, how schools and settings can avoid costly and stressful tribunals. Headteachers, teachers, SENCOs, Nursery Managers and anyone who works in educational settings will find this book essential to their professional development and a fantastic source of support and help.

Geraldine Hills is the founder and director of Inclusive Choice Consultancy, a training consultancy that provides Equality Act-related training to educators and other professionals, and is a guest lecturer at the University of Manchester.

Other titles published in association with the National Association for Special Educational Needs (nasen):

Forthcoming titles:

Language for Learning in the Secondary School: A Practical Guide for Supporting Students with Speech, Language and Communication Needs
Sue Hayden and Emma Jordan
2012/pb: 978-0-415-61975-2

ADHD: All Your Questions Answered: A Complete Handbook for SENCOs and Teachers
Fintan O'Regan
2012/pb: 978-0-415-59770-8

Assessing Children with Specific Learning Difficulties: A Teacher's Practical Guide
Gavin Reid, Gad Elbeheri and John Everatt
2012/pb: 978-0-415-67027-2

Using Playful Practice to Communicate with Special Children
Margaret Corke
2012/pb: 978-0-415-68767-6

The Equality Act for Educational Professionals: A Simple Guide to Disability Inclusion in Schools
Geraldine Hills
2012/pb: 978-0-415-68768-3

More Trouble with Maths: A Teacher's Complete Guide to Identifying and Diagnosing Mathematical Difficulties
Steve Chinn
2012/pb: 978-0-415-67013-5

Dyslexia and Inclusion: Classroom Approaches for Assessment, Teaching and Learning
Gavin Reid
2012/pb: 978-0-415-60758-2

Available now:

Brilliant Ideas for Using ICT in the Inclusive Classroom
Sally McKeown and Angela McGlashon
2011/pb: 978-0-415-67254-2

The SENCO Survival Guide: The Nuts and Bolts of Everything You Need to Know
Sylvia Edwards
2010/pb:978-0-415-59281-9

The SEN Handbook for Trainee Teachers, NQTs and Teaching Assistants
Wendy Spooner
2010/pb:978-0-415-56771-8

Attention Deficit Hyperactivity Disorder: What Can Teachers Do?
Geoff Kewley
2010/pb:978-0-415-49202-7

Young People with Anti-social Behaviours: Practical Resources for Professionals
Kathy Hampson
2010/pb: 978-0-415-56570-7

Confronting Obstacles to Inclusion: International Responses to Developing Inclusive Education
Richard Rose
2010/pb:978-0-415-49363-5

Supporting Children's Reading: A Complete Short Course for Teaching Assistants, Volunteer Helpers and Parents
Margaret Hughes and Peter Guppy
2010/pb: 978-0-415-49836-4

Dyspraxia 5–14: Identifying and Supporting Young People with Movement Difficulties
Christine Macintyre
2009/pb: 978-0-415-54396-5

A Handbook for Inclusion Managers: Steering your School towards Inclusion
Ann Sydney
2009/pb: 978-0-415-49198-3

Living with Dyslexia: The Social and Emotional Consequences of Specific Learning Difficulties/Disabilities
Barbara Riddick and Angela Fawcett
2009/pb: 978-0-415-47758-1

its
not the Altitude

THAT DEFINES

A PERSON'S SUCCESS

their
of
summit
the
its Attitude

The Equality Act for Educational Professionals

A simple guide to disability inclusion in schools

Geraldine Hills

Routledge
Taylor & Francis Group

LONDON AND NEW YORK

Helping Everyone Achieve

First published 2012
by Routledge
2 Park Square, Milton Park, Abingdon, Oxon OX14 4RN

Simultaneously published in the USA and Canada
by Routledge
711 Third Avenue, New York, NY 10017

Routledge is an imprint of the Taylor & Francis Group, an informa business

British Library Cataloguing in Publication Data
A catalogue record for this book is available from the British Library

Library of Congress Cataloging in Publication Data
Hills, Geraldine.
The Equality Act for educational professionals : a simple guide to disability inclusion in schools / Geraldine Hills.
p. cm.
Includes bibliographical references and index.
1. Children with disabilities–Education–Law and legislation–Great Britain. 2. Great Britain. Equality Act 2010. 3. Special education–Law and legislation–Great Britain. 4. Inclusive education–Great Britain.
5. Discrimination in education–Law and legislation–Great Britain. 6. Equality before the law–Great Britain. I. Title.
KD3663.H55 2012
344.41'0791–dc23
2011028140

ISBN: 978-0-415-68768-3 (pbk)
ISBN: 978-0-203-14040-6 (ebk)

Illustrations by Caron Stuart-Cole (stripyfish@live.com)
Typeset in Helvetica
by FiSH Books, Enfield

Printed and bound in Great Britain by the MPG Books Group

nasen is a professional membership association that supports all those who work with or care for children and young people with special and additional educational needs. Members include teachers, teaching assistants, support workers, other educationalists, students and parents.

nasen supports its members through policy documents, journals, its magazine Special!, publications, professional development courses, regional networks and newsletters. Its website contains more current information such as responses to government consultations. **nasen's** published documents are held in very high regard both in the UK and internationally.

Education is what remains when we have forgotten all that we have been taught.

George Savile, Marquis of Halifax

Dedication

This book is dedicated to Mr Brendan Hennessy, headteacher of St Cuthbert's RC Primary School in Manchester and all the wonderful staff there. Without their constant love and support for our son Sam and us as a family, we would not be where we are today. I am proud to have shared our son with this school.

A big thank you to 'beautiful Ms Yu' who kept us going when things felt so hard. You truly are a dedicated teaching assistant.

To Sam our son: we are so proud of you.

Contents

About the author		*xi*
Foreword		*xii*

1 Introduction — 1
Jargon busting — 1
Appreciative inquiry — 1
History of disability legislation — 2
Models of disability — 3
Definitions of disability and SEN — 6
Language — 9
Communication with people with disabilities — 9

2 Disability discrimination legislation — 12
The Equality Act 2010 — 12
Disability discrimination duties under the Equality Act — 12
Less favourable treatment of pupils with SEN and disabilities — 13
Reasonable adjustments — 19
Reasonable adjustments and the equality duty — 24
Treating people with disabilities more favourably — 26
Discrimination by association and perception — 28
Harassment — 28
Victimisation — 29

3 How the law affects school life — 32
The Equality Duty — 32
Admissions — 37
Exclusions — 39
Transport — 40
Managing medicines — 45
School trips — 46

4 Helping things get better — 51
Avoiding discrimination — 51
Information issues — 52
Busting the myths — 53
What can we do for parents? — 54
The responsible body — 56
The tribunal process — 56

5   And finally...   **61**
Some common misconceptions about the Equality Act   61
Commonly raised issues   61
The Codes of Practice   63
School improvement and the Equality Act   63

Postscript   **66**

Appendix 1: A quiz   **67**
Appendix 2: Suggested answers to case studies   **71**
Appendix 3: Disclosure letters   **78**

Index   *80*

About the author

Geraldine Hills is Inclusive Choice Consultancy's director. Geraldine has been working with people with disabilities for many years in various capacities. She has qualifications in teaching adults, and holds a BA in Learning Disability Studies from the Victoria University of Manchester. She is a guest lecturer within the education department at Manchester University and has carried out postgraduate research projects at the university. She has experience of the Special Educational Needs and Disability Tribunal (SEND) process, both as a volunteer for Independent Parental Special Educational Advice (IPSEA) and as a parent who successfully won a landmark tribunal for her child. She runs many courses for Manchester City Council as well as other local authorities and also works in collaboration with Sure Start children's centres where she is a consultant and trainer in the implementation of the Disability Equality Duty.

To get more information and to book a course, visit www.inclusivechoice.com.

Disclaimer

This book is intended to provide general guidance on the law. It does not constitute legal advice and is not an authoritative treatment of the law. Professional advice should be sought before acting on any of the material contained in this book as it may not be appropriate to your circumstances. This book is not intended to be used in place of reading the Codes of Practice or the Equality Act.

How to use this book

The main purpose of this book is to present the Equality Act in a user-friendly accessible way, and to encourage you to embrace these laws as something you are learning for yourself as well as others.

The book contains several case studies. These are designed for you to test your knowledge. Suggested answers to them can be found in Appendix 2. At the end of each chapter there is a list of documents and booklets that are available from the website that accompanies this book. These can be found at **www.inclusivechoice.com**, and are free to download. You will also find on the website details of courses and INSET training for your school. The Equality Act training course for schools complements this book and provides a solid foundation in disability legislation. This book contains many worked examples and case studies for discussion and can be used as a reference to ensure good inclusive practice is maintained in your school.

Foreword

It is fair to say that our laws that govern how we treat people and run our communities and organisations can often be complicated and perplexing, but often it is the underlying ideas, concepts and ethos of our laws that can be what it takes to fulfil our statutory duties.

As you work through this book you may be forgiven for thinking that the case studies are too simplistic or that the Equality Act, along with other associated Acts, is full of complicated reasoning and indigestible logic.

Well, I put before you another way of thinking about our discrimination laws and it is this: the more advanced medicine becomes the greater the chances are of us living longer. As we get older, the human body starts to deteriorate, which could then lead to disabilities such as reduced sight, hearing loss, mobility problems and communication difficulties. This is a sobering thought, especially when we then come to rely on services to help us maintain a good quality of life whilst retaining our self-esteem, dignity and independence. Then we come to rely greatly on our laws, in this case the Equality Act, to uphold our right to independence, choice and inclusion in our communities and the services it offers.

The Equality Act is not just for other people who have a disability; it's not just for the children you might teach or support; it's for you too. We all need to feel that we are living productive, interesting lives; to feel part of something, to feel included; and so we must ask ourselves when we are working towards understanding and implementing the duties within the Act, 'What would I want for myself?' I think you will find that we all want the same thing – to be treated with fairness and respect.

1 Introduction

Jargon busting

Learning a new subject is made much harder when you are faced with a barrage of acronyms. On the other hand, continuing to use the full name makes life difficult too. To get everyone on the same starting line, let's learn the acronyms right at the beginning:

Table 1.1 Acronyms.

EA	Equality Act
DDA	Disability Discrimination Act
EHRC	Equality and Human Rights Commission
SEN	Special Educational Needs
SENCO	SEN Co-ordinator
CRB	Criminal Records Bureau
SEND	SEN and Disability (Tribunal)
IPSEA	Independent Parental Special Education Advice
DED	Disability Equality Duty
DES	Disability Equality Scheme

Appreciative inquiry

This is the name of an approach that looks at issues in a different way. It asks us not to look for what is broken and fix it, but rather to look at what works. We approach our schools with an appreciative eye. It's not about looking at what we do through 'rose-tinted glasses' but about recognising our achievements.

For example, suppose you receive the results of a survey that was designed to assess parental satisfaction. It says that 94 per cent of your school's children's parents are happy with the service you provide. What would you normally do? You may decide to interview the 6 per cent that are unhappy. Appreciative inquiry says that you should ask the 94 per cent what you did to make them happy.

It is easy to view this as a rather simplistic way to face the school's biggest challenges, but it is also easy to be cynical and dismissive of this approach. We should encourage a working environment of appreciation of what works, which will then lead to a positive shift in attitudes. At the end of your next meeting, try asking this simple question: 'What did we do well in this meeting?'

As you read this book, remember all the good practices your school already has. Remember the successful outcomes you have achieved for all your pupils with SEN and disabilities, no matter how small these might have been. Use this information to perform an appreciative enquiry into your inclusive practice, as these will be your building blocks for future successful outcomes.

History of disability legislation

From October 2010, the Equality Act (EA) came into force. This book explains how the EA applies to those providing education in schools. It provides examples of how the duties work and suggests some simple approaches that may help to ensure that children with disabilities are not discriminated against.

The largest single change in disability legislation happened when the Disability Discrimination Act was introduced in 1995. This made it unlawful to discriminate against people in respect of their disabilities in relation to employment, the provision of goods and services, education and transport. In addition to imposing obligations on employers, the Act placed duties on service providers and required 'reasonable adjustments' to be made when providing access to goods, facilities, services and premises.

In 1996 it became unlawful for service providers to treat people with disabilities less favourably for a reason related to their disability (termed 'Less Favourable Treatment'). In 2001, the Special Educational Needs and Disability Act extended the DDA to cover education. In 2003, people who are registered as blind or partially sighted were automatically deemed as being disabled for DDA purposes. In 2004, part 3, which deals with organisations offering services, was amended to ensure service providers made reasonable adjustments to physical features of their premises to overcome barriers to access. In 2005, the scope of the DDA was extended to cover people with HIV, cancer and multiple sclerosis.

The Disability Discrimination Act 2005 brought in the Disability Equality Duty for all public authorities. In addition, specific duties, which include the development of a disability equality scheme, apply to some public authorities. Public bodies and local authorities are included in the specific duties. These duties apply to the provision made by organisations and local authorities but also need to be taken into account when organisations and local authorities procure goods and services from other agencies to whom the duties may not apply; for example, where service provision is run by a voluntary organisation or a private company.

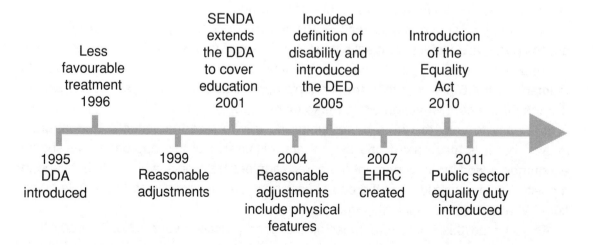

Figure 1.1 Timeline of recent disability legislation

In 2007, the Disability Rights Commission was subsumed into the Equality and Human Rights Commission (EHRC). The EHRC has powers to issue guidance on and enforce all the equality enactments (covering race, sex, disability, religion and belief, sexual orientation and age).

In 2010, the Equality Act was introduced, which combined discrimination and equality law for race, sex, disability, religion and belief, sexual orientation and age into one single act.

A new fundamental principle

The Disability Discrimination Act 1995 departed from the fundamental principles of older UK discrimination law (the Sex Discrimination Act 1975 and the Race Relations Act 1976). These acts depended on the concepts of 'direct discrimination' and 'indirect discrimination'. However, those concepts were deemed insufficient to deal with the issues of disability discrimination. The core concepts in the DDA 1995 were, instead:

- 'less favourable treatment' for a reason related to a person's disability;
- failure to make a 'reasonable adjustment'.

'Reasonable adjustment' is the radical concept that made the DDA so different. Instead of 'indirect discrimination', where someone can take action if they have been disadvantaged by a policy or practice, reasonable adjustment is an active approach that requires employers, schools and service providers to take steps to remove barriers from participation by disabled people. The concept is retained in the new Equality Act.

Models of disability

Trying to understand human intelligence has been a preoccupation of many scientists and psychologists since antiquity. There is nothing new in trying to pigeonhole people, whether it's the way we dress, where we live or what our political persuasion might be. The need to identify who we are and what we are capable of is part of being human. We all have labels given to us whether we like it or not – fat, slim, black, white, clever or stupid. Putting people into groups is a very human practice, but when labelling becomes a matter of political policy, when those labels stop you from fulfilling your potential in life, when doors are closed to you due to unfair and biased labelling, then it is time to reassess and account for our attitudes and open ourselves up to new ways of thinking.

The medical model of disability

The medical model promotes the view of a person with a disability as dependent and needing to be cured or cared for, and it justifies the way in which people with disabilities have been systematically excluded from society. The person with the disability is the problem, not society. Control resides firmly with professionals; choices for the individual are limited to the options provided and approved by the 'helping' expert. The medical model, naturally enough, concentrates on disease and impairments. It puts what is wrong with someone in the foreground. It is concerned with causes of disease. It defines and categorises conditions, distinguishes different forms and assesses severities.

Figure 1.2 Labels.

However, there is a place for the medical model in school, and that is to help understand a pupil's medical needs, i.e. medication and emergency procedures. It should not be used to predict how the child will fare within the school environment.

The medical model is sometimes known as the 'individual model' because it promotes the notion that it is the individual person who must adapt to the way in which society is constructed and organised.

Powerful and pervasive views of people with disabilities are reinforced in the media, books, films, comics, art and language. Many people with disabilities internalise negative views of themselves that create feelings of low self-esteem and achievement. The 'medical model' shows people with disabilities in a negative light and creates a cycle of dependency and exclusion, which is difficult to break. The 'medical model' thinking often predominates in schools where special educational needs are thought of as resulting from the individual, who is seen as different, faulty, and needing to be assessed and made as normal as possible. If people were to start from the point of view of all children's right to belong and be valued in their local school we would start by looking at what is wrong with the school and the strengths of the child.

What is unhelpful about the medical model?

It is likely to inspire pity or even fear. Pity is not a useful emotion. Many people are scared of impairments, sometimes irrationally so. The medical model risks objectifying people, lumping them together because of their condition, not because of who they are. Perhaps the most important consequence of the medical model is that bringing the impairment into the foreground risks pushing the person into the background. They become less of a person and more a collection of symptoms. What is more, it doesn't have very much to say about people's lives and how they live them.

The social model

This second approach is based on the social model of disability. The social model of disability is a different way of thinking about disability. It is often said that a big part of the battle to overcome the barriers faced by people with disabilities has to do with changing 'hearts and minds'. The idea is to replace old-style thinking with a very different perspective. The aim is to help people to *see the person first, not the disability*. That helps remove much of the fear and anxiety that people have about disability, and can clarify what changes need to be made in society.

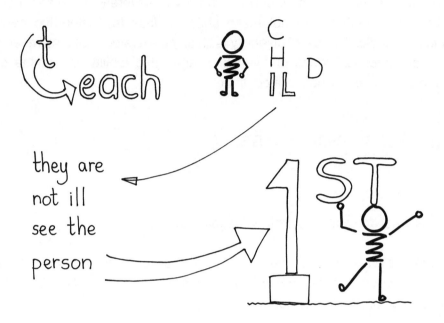

Figure 1.3 See the person first.

Instead of emphasising the disability, the social model puts the person at the forefront. It emphasises dignity, independence, choice and privacy. Words are important, not because of the need to use the fashionably correct terms, but because the terminology reveals the thinking behind them. Here are some definitions of two key words:

> **Impairment**. Having an impairment means there is something not working properly with part of the body, mind or senses. Someone who has had a leg amputated has an impairment; so does someone whose learning disability makes it difficult for them to remember things; so does someone who is partially blind, or deaf, or who has epileptic seizures, or who has unwanted muscular spasms, or any number of things that don't work properly.

> **Disability** occurs when a person is excluded, because of their impairment, from something that other people in society take for granted. That might be the chance to attend an event, access some service or get involved in an activity in a school setting. To challenge discrimination against people with disabilities, we must begin in our schools.

Why is a social model of disability needed?

The standard way of thinking about disability in the past was the medical model. That remains fine for doctors but it is less useful for others and is mostly unhelpful when applied in our schools. Some schools still see the child through the medical model and lay the problem of inclusion firmly with the child and their disability. When schools work from a social model perspective, they look closely at the school environment, their attitude and overall image of disability. They realise that understanding and embracing the social model helps change our attitudes, dispels myths and creates good solid foundations for our children with SEN and abilities to thrive in school.

The fight for the inclusion of all children, however 'severely' disabled, in one, mainstream, education system, will not make sense unless the difference between the 'social' and the 'medical' model of disability is clearly understood. Unless we address our own fears, preconceived ideas or even bias against disability, discrimination in our schools and society as a whole will continue.

Definitions of disability and SEN

Disability

In the Equality Act, 'disability' is defined as follows:

> *A person has a disability for the purposes of this Act if he has a physical or mental impairment which has a substantial and long-term adverse effect on his ability to carry out normal day-to-day activities.*

There is a common misunderstanding that the EA covers only people who have a sensory or physical impairment. The breadth of the EA definition arises from the breadth of the terms:

- **substantial**, defined as *more than minor or trivial*;
- **long-term**, defined as *a year or more*.

The test of whether impairment affects normal day-to-day activity is whether it affects one or more of the following: mobility; manual dexterity; physical co-ordination; continence; ability to lift, carry or otherwise move everyday objects; speech, hearing or eyesight; memory or ability to concentrate, learn or understand; or the perception of risk of physical danger.

The EA also covers people with:

- severe disfigurements;
- impairments that are controlled or corrected by the use of medication, prostheses, or other aids (excluding spectacles);
- progressive symptomatic conditions;
- cancer, HIV or multiple sclerosis at the point of diagnosis.

However, the EA does not cover addiction to or dependence on nicotine, tobacco or other non-prescribed drugs or substances; hay fever; or certain mental illnesses that have antisocial consequences. Accordingly, it might be possible for a pupil to have special educational needs but not be disabled for the purposes of the EA, and *vice versa* (although the majority of pupils with disabilities will also have some special educational needs).

Special educational needs (SEN)

Not all children who are defined as disabled will have SEN. For example, those with severe asthma, arthritis or diabetes may not have SEN but may have rights under the EA. The Equality and Human Rights Commission's Code of Practice for Schools is helpful in explaining this in more detail.

The Department for Education defines children with SEN as:

Having learning difficulties or disabilities which make it harder for them to learn or access education than most other children of the same age.

Children have a learning difficulty if they:

a. *Have a significantly greater difficulty in learning than the majority of children of the same age; or*
b. *Have a disability which prevents or hinders them from making use of educational facilities of a kind generally provided for children of the same age in schools within the area of the local education authority;*
c. *Are under compulsory school age and fall within the definition at (a) or (b) above or would so do if special educational provision was not made for them.*

Children are not regarded as having a learning difficulty solely because they are not being taught in their first language.

Hidden impairments

Hidden impairments are those that might not be immediately obvious, but they are also covered under the definition of disability. Many people with hidden impairments may not feel their needs are recognised, or appropriate support provided, to enable them to participate in mainstream education. This is why it is important for schools to build good partnerships with parents to encourage the disclosure of any hidden impairments their child may have. Of course, the school may also seek input from the child also.

Hidden impairments may manifest for pupils when trying to access a learning resource, such as the school library or IT facilities. This could be difficult for pupils with dyslexia because it may take longer than other children to find books, write notes or find appropriate sections to photocopy. It may also be more difficult for them to retain information once they have read it. Making sure pupils (and their parents) are aware that there are computers set aside with assistive software will encourage parental disclosure and better inclusion for pupils with some hidden impairments.

Examples of some hidden impairments include:

● attention deficit hyperactivity disorder (ADHD);
● dyslexia;

- autism;
- physical co-ordination;
- incontinence;
- ability to lift, carry or otherwise move everyday objects;
- speech, hearing or eyesight (unless correctable by spectacles);
- memory or ability to concentrate, learn or understand;
- perception of risk of physical danger.

It is important to note that it will never be for a school to decide whether a child is disabled. Only a court or the SEND tribunal can do this, so you should seek further information from families and pupils to ensure that you find out about any hidden impairments the child may have.

SEN, disabled or both?

Though the definition of disability comes from the EA and the definition of SEN comes from the Education Act 1996, there is a significant overlap between the two groups of children (see Figure 1.4).

A child may fall within one or more of the definitions.

Figure 1.4 gives some indication as to possible differences between SEN and EA definitions of disability for children and young people. However, each case needs to be judged on the impact on the day-to-day life of the person.

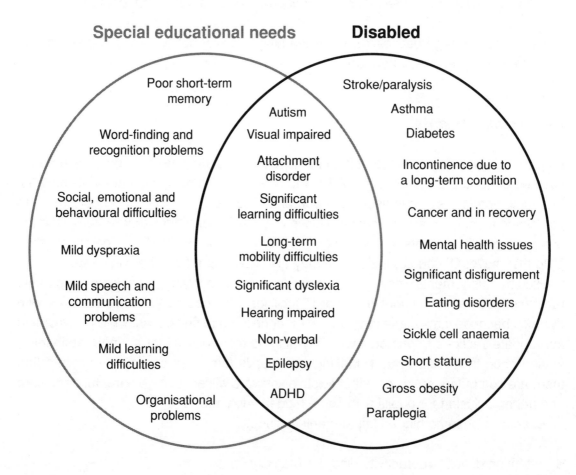

Figure 1.4 SEN, disabled, or both?

Language

Any member of your staff who comes into contact with members of the public should treat everyone they come across with dignity and respect. This will help you provide good service (not just without unlawfully discriminating, but more generally) and can make children and parents less likely to complain.

Some people see the use of 'politically correct' language as a ridiculous thing and annoying when they are picked up on it. Although it can, and sometimes is, taken to ridiculous extremes, if certain words or terms are offensive to people with disabilities, why would we choose to continue to use them when there are perfectly valid alternatives?

Although you may see yourself as tolerant and not discriminatory, the first time you meet a person with a disability they will not know that about you and may judge you on how you treat them straight away. For this reason, being careful with your language will create a much better first impression.

There are certain words that, today, have quite negative connotations. Try to avoid words like: handicapped, crippled, retarded, invalid, sufferer. Remember that you should see the person first, not the disability. Therefore terms such as 'the disabled' are not helpful. Grouping people with disabilities all together is never helpful, since all people with disabilities are individuals with different difficulties, outlooks, opinions, ways of life and ambitions. It would be the same as grouping everyone with blue eyes together – when did you last use the term 'the blue-eyed'!

In the same way, defining or referring to people by the condition or disability they have makes an unnecessary grouping of people who are only similar in one way.

Avoid the term 'normal'. Saying 'normal people' or 'normal schools' when you mean non-disabled people just marks people with disabilities as being 'abnormal'. As you age and become hard of hearing, would you consider yourself 'abnormal' or would just 'hard of hearing' be a more appropriate description?

If in doubt, ask the person. It is quite common to feel uncomfortable sometimes, and the person with the disability probably realises that, so just ask them how they would like to be addressed or treated. After all, what would you want for yourself or your own child?

Communication with people with disabilities

For some people, dealing with a person with a disability for the first time can be difficult and uncomfortable. The following sections give some advice on how to communicate with people with certain disabilities.

Communication with people with a visual impairment

Even with the best intentions, it is a mistake to think that someone with a visual impairment automatically will need help. Having a visual impairment does not equate to helplessness. People with a visual impairment may not be able to do everything in the same way as other people, but we all have limitations and we all need support in different areas of our lives. No matter what the disability, approaching any situation from a social model perspective and asking yourself 'What reasonable adjustment can I put in place in my setting' will go a long way to successful inclusion.

Bust some myths...

- It is not necessary to raise your voice when speaking to a visually impaired person.
- Do not assume a visually impaired person can't do something simply because they are visually impaired or blind. If you want to know you can always ask.
- Blindness does not automatically ensure that other senses will be improved. Any sensory development will take time and awareness to develop. It doesn't happen because the person can't see.
- Don't worry about saying the words 'watch' or 'see' in sentences.
- There is no such thing as a dumb question except the one you don't ask.
- Every person who is blind is different. Each person you will meet probably has a different type of vision loss and probably sees things differently. Some are more capable than others. You should keep your expectations as high as you would for any pupil.

For more interesting anecdotes, see: http://www.dealingwithvisionloss.com/Excerpts/MeetingABlindPersonExcerpt.aspx

Communication with people with a hearing impairment

People with a hearing impairment may be able to speak so well as to be almost hearing... or may have such a limited amount of language that they can only communicate with very basic gestures. The point is that not everyone is the same. The person with a hearing impairment you meet at work may be quite different to your grandfather who is gradually losing his hearing. Do not assume that someone with a hearing impairment can sign or lip-read.

The following tips will help prepare you to deal with communication with people with a hearing impairment. Try to have patience, as it will, in almost all cases, take longer to have a conversation.

- The first thing is to ask the pupil or parent how they prefer to communicate, whether it be lip-reading, writing or signing.
- To facilitate lip-reading, make sure there is plenty of light. If you are outside in the daytime, make sure there is some kind of shade so that the glare from the sun isn't an obstacle.
- To attract a deaf pupil's attention, you can either wave your hand or tap their shoulders gently.
- If you are a male, be aware that your facial hair can have a dramatic influence on your communication with the deaf person. Some people can lip-read a person with a moustache and beard; others may find it very difficult.
- Do not shout. In most cases, this doesn't work.
- Try to minimize the amount of background noise. Make sure your face is in plain view. If the pupil shows signs of being confused, ask if they understood what you said and repeat your statements if necessary.
- If you normally speak very softly, try to speak louder. If you usually speak quickly, slow down.
- For most deaf people, communicating on a one-to-one level is much easier than in a group situation. When you are doing group class work, try to cue the pupil from

time to time what is occurring. Take the time to write good notes and share them with the pupil. Ask if they understood what was happening and if they needed clarification on any points.

For more interesting anecdotes, see: http://www.his.com/~lola/deaf.html

Communication with pupils with speech impairments

It can be difficult sometimes to talk to a pupil with a speech impairment. These simple guidelines will help them feel valued and ensure better communication in the classroom.

- Listen patiently.
- Don't finish sentences unless asked to. Hear them out and don't interrupt.
- Do not try to play guessing games as to what you think they might be saying.
- Don't pretend to understand.
- Summarise, to check understanding.
- Remember that the ability or inability to speak is not a measure of intelligence; it is only the speech that is impaired.
- Don't be afraid to ask them to repeat what they said.

For more interesting anecdotes, see: http://www.associatedcontent.com/article/52459/5_tips_for_talking_to_someone_with.html

Additional resources

These booklets can be found on the Inclusive Choice website:

- Code of Practice for Schools
- Disability Discrimination Act 1995
- Duties and Definitions
- Early Years and the Disability Discrimination Act
- Including Me – managing complex health needs in schools and early years settings
- SEN Code of Practice
- The Medical and Social Models of Disability
- The Social Model of Disability
- Using Disability Models to Understand how Schools Create Bullying

2 Disability discrimination legislation

The Equality Act 2010

In 2010, the Equality Act was introduced to codify the complicated and numerous array of Acts and Regulations that formed the basis of anti-discrimination law in Great Britain. This was, primarily, the Equal Pay Act 1970, the Sex Discrimination Act 1975, the Race Relations Act 1976, the Disability Discrimination Act 1995 and three major statutory instruments protecting discrimination in employment on grounds of religion or belief, sexual orientation and age.

The Equality Act defines eight 'Protected Characteristics' for people who use services. These are:

1 age
2 disability
3 gender reassignment
4 pregnancy and maternity
5 race
6 religion and belief
7 sex (gender)
8 sexual orientation.

This book concentrates on the legislation governing disability, since this will have most effect on schools.

Disability discrimination duties under the Equality Act

The Equality Act makes it illegal to discriminate against a person with a disability for a reason related to their disability. It also makes it illegal to have rules, policies or practices that apply to everyone but which particularly disadvantage people with disabilities. Your school is required to make *reasonable adjustments* to allow children with disabilities to fully partake in the activities of your school. These requirements can be encapsulated into the two duties inherited from the Disability Discrimination Act:

Less favourable treatment

Children with disabilities are entitled not to be treated less favourably than non-disabled children for a reason relating to their disability, without reasonable justification.

Reasonable adjustments

Children with disabilities are entitled to have reasonable adjustments made with respect to admission arrangements or in the provision of education and associated services, to prevent them being placed at a substantial disadvantage, unless the refusal to make those adjustments can be justified.

Less favourable treatment of pupils with SEN and disabilities

To decide whether a school has treated a pupil less favourably, a comparison must be made with how it would have treated other pupils in similar circumstances. If the school's treatment of the pupil puts them at a clear disadvantage compared with other pupils, then it is likely that the treatment will be less favourable. Less favourable treatment could also involve being deprived of a choice or being excluded.

If the quality of the education, benefit, facility or service being offered, or even the manner in which it is offered, is comparatively poor, this could also amount to less favourable treatment.

Figure 2.1 Partnership working.

This is best understood with examples.

Example

A parent seeks admission to a school for her child who has a bowel disease. The school says that it cannot admit him until he is toilet trained. That is their policy for all children. Some bowel diseases may lead to the late establishment of bowel control. The refusal to admit the child is for a reason related to his disability and may be discriminatory. There may sometimes be justification for less favourable treatment, but it is the blanket policy in this example that is likely to make it discriminatory.

Example _____

A pupil with autism goes to the front of the dinner queue. A teacher standing nearby tells him not to 'barge in'. The pupil becomes anxious but does not move. The teacher insists that the pupil must not 'jump the queue'. The pupil becomes more anxious and agitated and hits the teacher. The pupil is excluded temporarily from the school.

1   Was there any less favourable treatment?
2   Is the less favourable treatment for a reason related to the pupil's disability?

The reason for the exclusion – hitting the teacher – may be related to the pupil's disability. Particular features of his autism may be that he has difficulty in managing social situations, he has difficulty in understanding the purpose of a queue, he has difficulty in understanding figurative language, such as 'barge in' and 'jump the queue', or he has difficulty in managing escalating levels of anxiety. If the hitting is related to these features of his autism, then the less favourable treatment, the exclusion, is for a reason related to the pupil's disability. This is likely to be viewed as disability discrimination.

Following on from the two previous examples of less favourable treatment, have a go at Case study 1.

Case study 1

A pupil with Tourette's syndrome is admitted to a school. The school wants the pupil to have all their lessons in a separate room in case they distract other children with their involuntary noises and body movements.

    The reasons for placing the pupil in a separate room are the involuntary noises and body movements. These are an intrinsic part of their disability.

    The school also claims that the inclusion of the pupil is causing significant disadvantage for the provision of efficient education for other children.

    Is the less favourable treatment related to the child's disability?

A suggested answer can be found on page 71.

The concept of less favourable treatment encapsulates three forms of discrimination that are defined in the Equality Act. In practice, it is not important to know the names of the various different types of discrimination, just that they are all illegal.

Direct discrimination

This is discrimination directly related to the child's disability – for example, not allowing a child with a disfigurement to appear in a play because of their looks. Direct discrimination is unlawful, irrespective of the school's motive or intention, and regardless of whether the less favourable treatment of the child is conscious or unconscious.

    Sometimes it can be our own attitudes and beliefs that are prejudiced and need adjustment. Direct discrimination can only be avoided in our schools if we are willing to accept that, no matter how good our intentions are, we may have ideas or beliefs about disability that may cause us to treat pupils with disabilities differently.

Example

A teacher decides to deny a pupil with a facial disfigurement a place on the school debating team because he believes other pupils taking part in the debates will make fun of him and cause him upset. Although the teacher may be well-intentioned, denying the pupil a chance to be on the team is likely to be direct disability discrimination.

From the Code of Practice for Schools

Discrimination arising from disability

This is discrimination for a reason *connected* to the child's disability. For example, a school nursery requiring all children to be toilet trained before being admitted to the nursery may discriminate against a child with a disability that causes them not to have full bowel control. Discrimination arising from disability has occurred when a child with a disability is treated:

- less favourably than another child;
- for a reason related to the child's disability;
- when it cannot be justified.

Indirect discrimination

Indirect discrimination occurs when a school puts in place rules, policies or practices that apply to all children, but which particularly disadvantage children with disabilities. If the school cannot show that the policy or practice is justified as a *proportionate* means of achieving a legitimate aim, then this may well amount to indirect discrimination towards the disabled pupil.

Example

A school playground has a variety of adventure play equipment. On health and safety grounds, it has concerns that pupils with physical impairments will not be able to use the equipment without significant financial expenditure, so it makes a decision to prohibit these pupils from using the equipment.

Although ensuring health and safety is a legitimate aim, the blanket application of the policy is likely to be unjustified if pupils with disabilities would be able to use the equipment with a few modifications for a moderate cost.

In a case involving disability, if the school has not complied with its duty to make relevant reasonable adjustments, it will be difficult for the school to show that the treatment was *proportionate*.

From the Code of Practice for Schools

Is there less favourable treatment that can be justified?

The Act says that less favourable treatment that is justified is not unlawful discrimination. There are two ways in which less favourable treatment may be justified under the Act:

- If it is the result of a permitted form of selection on ability or aptitude. Some local authorities allow selective schools, which have admission criteria based on ability.
- If there is a reason that is both material to the circumstances of the particular case and substantial. For example, if a pupil is required to make a speech to a potential donor, you may be justified in not choosing a pupil who has a severe speech impediment.

'A proportionate means of achieving a legitimate aim'

If the school has treated a pupil or group of pupils less favourably, then if it can show that their actions are 'a proportionate means of achieving a legitimate aim', then it will not amount to discrimination. This is often known as the *objective justification test*.

If challenged in a tribunal, the school must justify the action it has taken. It is up to the school to produce evidence to support its assertion that it was justified. Generalisations are not sufficient to provide justification. The question of whether the action is a proportionate means of achieving a legitimate aim is approached in two stages:

- Is the aim of the action legal and non-discriminatory, and one that represents a real, objective consideration?
- If the aim is legitimate, is the means of achieving it proportionate – that is appropriate and necessary in all the circumstances?

Economic efficiency is not a legitimate aim. For example, the school cannot simply argue that to discriminate is cheaper than not to discriminate. Examples of legitimate aims include:

- ensuring that education, benefits, facilities and services are targeted at those who most need them;
- ensuring the health and safety of pupils and staff (provided risks are clearly specified);
- maintaining academic and behaviour standards;
- ensuring the well-being and dignity of pupils.

The definition of what is proportionate is covered in more detail on page 27.

Example

An exchange trip is offered to pupils studying Italian in a secondary school. Accessible transport arrangements are made and a suitable host is identified who can accommodate a pupil who uses a wheelchair.

However, at the last minute the Italian host drops out. There is no time to make any other reasonable adjustment. The school decides to go ahead with the trip, but tells the child with the disability he can no longer go.

The school considers the following options:

a. it is not practicable to take the pupil with the disability without a host to go to;
b. the school considers cancelling the trip, but if the other pupils do not go, they will lose the opportunity of improving their Italian.

From the Code of Practice for Schools

In the interests of other pupils, the school decides to go ahead with the trip. The school has considered the relevant factors, and whilst it has not been able to identify a reasonable adjustment that would enable the pupil to go on the trip, it is likely to be acting lawfully as it has done all that it reasonably could to include the pupil. Nevertheless, the school should try to make alternative provision so that the pupil still has the opportunity to improve his/her Italian in an interesting and enjoyable way.

It is important to understand that, although in this case the school has not acted unlawfully, schools have a duty to be proactive and to 'anticipate' the likely needs of current and future pupils on school visits, and should not respond reactively or retrospectively. It would have been reasonable to expect the school to have had a back-up plan, as they might if a member of staff were to fall ill at the last moment.

Example

A child attending his local mainstream school has speech and language difficulties and exhibits challenging behaviour. Throughout his schooling he has been inclined to kick and lash out, turn over tables and chairs, damage work and throw objects, including, on one occasion, a pair of scissors.

Other pupils have to be kept out of the way and on at least one occasion his class teacher has been scratched and kicked by him. His behaviour book records some incidents where he has hurt other children and himself. The school felt that it had no alternative but to temporarily exclude the child.

The child's parent has claimed that the school unlawfully discriminated against their son with regards to less favourable treatment and claimed that no *reasonable adjustments* were made in order to make sure the exclusion did not take place.

The school was able to produce evidence to support its assertion that it is justified in the exclusion of the child. The school was able to produce reports on advice received and input from the local authority's behavioural support service since the child's admission to the school. Other professionals have also contributed to his programmes, including educational psychologists and the local authority's behavioural and specialist SEN support services.

The important point here is that the school was able to show the tribunal a document trail of extra support. The school was also able to show detailed behavioural management techniques utilised, programmes including reward systems that had been effective and efforts to encourage continuation of these techniques at home.

The headteacher and the experienced learning support assistant gave details of the provision put in place for the child by the school and his progress since he arrived. They mentioned procedures they followed and agencies and persons from whom they took advice. The school produced copies of the home/school liaison material to show how they had worked to build up a good relationship with home.

In this case a tribunal may find that the school did not discriminate unlawfully against the child. This would be mainly due to the school's well-documented account of all the reasonable adjustments it had put in place and of the outside agencies it had worked with in order to provide best practices for the child.

Permitted forms of selection

Although permitted forms of selection can be seen as less favourable treatment that is justified, and therefore not unlawful discrimination, schools should make sure that they have done all they can to gather information about any pupils with disabilities that may be sitting the school's entrance exam.

Example

A grammar school considers carefully how children with disabilities can take their entrance exams without being at a substantial disadvantage. As part of its reasonable adjustments duty, the school sets up early admissions meetings with the parents of prospective pupils with disabilities. The meetings are used to discuss any special arrangements for the exams. The particular arrangements for an individual child can then be put in place in time. This would be a reasonable adjustment for the school to make.

From the Code of Practice for Schools

Case study 2

An 11-year-old girl with learning difficulties applies to go to a school that selects its intake on the basis of academic ability. She fails the entrance test. She is refused admission.

1   Was there less favourable treatment?
2   If so, was the less favourable treatment justified?
3   If so, why was it justified?

Suggested answers can be found on page 71.

Case study 3

A school has received a number of complaints from local shopkeepers about the rowdy and disruptive behaviour of some of its pupils. It decides that the pupils in question should be banned from taking part in a school theatre visit because of their behaviour. One of the pupils has a hearing impairment.

1   Was there less favourable treatment by the school?
2   Can it be justified?

From the Code of Practice for Schools

Suggested answers can be found on page 72.

Note that the concept of less favourable treatment does not mean that children with disabilities have an excuse for disruptive or antisocial behaviour. There has to be a direct relationship between the reason for the less favourable treatment and the child's disability.

Reasonable adjustments

The good news, for most schools at least, is that you are implementing reasonable adjustments every day, maybe without even knowing it. A reasonable adjustment does not have to be something that is done on a grand scale, and which costs lots of money; it can be in the little things you do every day, such as placing a hearing-impaired child at the front of the class, or asking a parent what sort of things they do at home to help their child. It could be asking the pupil what makes things easier for them, thinking about lighting, the language you use or adjusting your own attitude.

Figure 2.2 Turn fear into hear.

The Equality Act *requires* your school and your local authority to make reasonable adjustments to ensure that pupils with disabilities are not at a substantial disadvantage. Reasonable adjustments meet the statutory requirements when they:

● act to prevent pupils with disabilities being placed at a substantial disadvantage;
● are aimed at all pupils with a disability;
● are anticipatory;
● enable pupils to participate in education and associated services.

The Act does not specify what factors should be taken into account when considering whether or not a step is a 'reasonable' one to take. The Code of Practice for Schools states that what is reasonable will vary according to:

● the type of service being provided;
● the nature of the service provider and its size and resources;
● how the person's disability affects them in that context.

The Code also says that some of the following factors might be taken into account when considering what is reasonable:

- how effective any steps would be in overcoming the difficulty that people with disabilities face in accessing the services;
- how practicable it would be for the school to take these steps;
- how disruptive taking the steps would be;
- the financial and other costs of making the adjustment;
- the extent of the service provider's financial and other resources;
- the amount of any resources already spent on making adjustments;
- the availability of financial or other assistance.

Let's revisit the example on page 14 of the boy who hit the teacher and was excluded. The less favourable treatment (exclusion) is likely to be justified in terms of the order and discipline in the school. Any assault is likely to be a 'material and substantial' reason justifying exclusion.

However, there may be reasonable steps that might have been taken to prevent the incident happening in the first place. For staff, there might have been training about autism and how the disability manifests itself; on strategies to avoid difficulties, for example, avoiding negative instructions and symbolic language such as 'barging in' and 'jumping the queue', and on strategies to overcome difficulties if they do arise. For the pupil, there might have been training for social situations, such as queuing, and the development of strategies for communicating that he is upset or confused.

If reasonable steps of this type could have been taken but were not, it may be difficult for the school to justify the exclusion. If steps of this type *were* taken but the incident still happened, the school is likely to be able to justify the exclusion.

The key to making reasonable adjustments is thinking ahead – anticipating barriers and how to remove them to enable a child with a disability to join in, enjoy an activity and benefit from it. To do this effectively it is necessary to involve parents and children in sharing information and thinking creatively. Parents may already have encountered similar barriers and found effective ways of removing or minimising them.

Example

Two children with hearing impairments are going to be admitted to a school. Some typical reasonable adjustments the school might make include:

- arranging training for staff in the appropriate use of hearing radio aids;
- drawing up guidance for staff in the light of the training, which may include guidance on the use of radio microphones, the transfer of microphones to other children at group times, and checking that the children's aids are set correctly for different activities;
- deciding to change the location of the book corner so that at story times and other times when the children come together as a group, natural light illuminates the face, mouth and gestures of the staff talking to the children;
- paying particular attention to having visual prompts to hand when planning activities with the children and using puppets and other props at story times.

Key factors for success in making reasonable adjustments

Vision and values based on an inclusive ethos

An inclusive vision for the school, clearly articulated, shared, understood and acted upon effectively by all, is an important factor in enabling staff to make reasonable adjustments.

A 'can-do' attitude from all staff

The attitude of staff is fundamental to achieving successful outcomes for pupils with disabilities. Where staff are positive and demonstrate a 'can-do' approach, barriers are more easily overcome.

A proactive approach to identifying barriers and finding practical solutions

Actively identifying barriers as early as possible and exploring solutions using a practical, problem-solving approach has led schools to identify more effective reasonable adjustments.

Strong collaborative relationships with pupils and parents

Schools that are effective at making reasonable adjustments recognise that parents and pupils have expertise about living with an impairment and will be a major source of advice. Pupils can also be the best judges of what is effective. They can be good advocates for what has worked well for them.

A meaningful voice for pupils

Schools are more likely to make effective reasonable adjustments where there are strong consultative mechanisms in place for all pupils and where peer support is well-developed.

A positive approach to managing behaviour

Combined with an appropriate curriculum and a variety of learning activities, a positive approach to managing behaviour can enable pupils to take charge of their own behaviour and support others in taking charge of theirs. Many schools identified the importance of peer support strategies and of mentoring schemes in developing a positive approach to challenging behaviour.

Strong leadership by senior management and governors

Strong school leadership that sets a clear direction, promotes positive outcomes for pupils with disabilities, deploys the resources of the school to support teachers in identifying and removing barriers and keeps progress under review, makes for schools that are more effective at making reasonable adjustments.

Effective staff training and development

Where staff training and development is given a high priority, it can ensure that staff have the understanding, knowledge and skills required to make reasonable adjustments for the range of pupils with disabilities.

The use of expertise from outside the school

Other agencies supplement and complement what a school can provide on its own. Schools may draw on a wide range of expertise beyond the school: from other local schools, units and support services; from different statutory agencies; and from voluntary organisations.

Building disability into resourcing arrangements

Building disability considerations into everything a school does, including the way it deploys its resources, enables everyone in the school to make reasonable adjustments.

A sensitive approach to meeting the impairment-specific needs of pupils

A sensitive approach protects the dignity of pupils with disabilities, particularly in relation to meeting medical and personal care needs. Reasonable adjustments should not highlight any negative effects on the rest of the class so as to cause any resentment of the pupil with the disability.

Regular critical review and evaluation

Regular reviews at pupil level, departmental level and school level help to ensure that:

● progress is monitored;
● successes and failures are shared and inform the next steps;
● the views of pupils and their parents are sought and incorporated into the reasonable adjustments the school makes.

The availability of role models and positive images of disability across the school

Where schools use a range of opportunities to provide role models with disabilities, both children and adults, this can boost the self-esteem of pupils with disabilities and have a positive effect for all pupils. This can be supported by positive images of children and adults with disabilities in pictures, books and a range of materials used in schools.

Case study 4

A boy with Down's Syndrome had been attending a mainstream secondary school successfully. Following an annual review, it was agreed that a teaching assistant should support the boy in some of his lessons. One of the boy's subject teachers claimed that having another adult in the classroom would be disruptive and make the child's inclusion incompatible with the efficient education of other children. The school therefore argued that it could not continue to provide mainstream education for that pupil.

1 Was the school justified in its actions?
2 If not, what reasonable steps could the school have taken?

Suggested answers can be found on page 72.

It can be useful to use a checklist to ensure your reasonable adjustments duties are suitable. An example checklist is shown in Table 2.2.

Table 2.2 Reasonable adjustments checklist.

General duties to disabled pupils	Yes	No	Evidence
Does the governing body receive regular reports on how your school is meeting its duties to pupils with disabilities: ● to ensure appropriate provision is made? ● not to treat less favourably? ● to make reasonable adjustments? ● to draw up and implement an accessibility plan?			
Does the governing body report annually to parents on how your school is meeting its duties?			
Is the governing body aware of how many pupils with disabilities there are in your school?			
Reasonable adjustments			
Do you make reasonable adjustments to your policies on admissions, education and associated services and exclusions, for pupils with disabilities and prospective pupils?			
Do you keep your policies, practices and procedures under review to ensure you are not discriminating?			
Are all staff aware of the need to make reasonable adjustments: managers, teaching staff, learning support assistants, catering staff, caretakers and others?			
Does the governing body have evidence of the participation of pupils with disabilities across the life of your school?			
Does the governing body have evidence of the outcomes for pupils with disabilities across the life of your school?			
Does the governing body know what the views of pupils with disabilities and their parents are?			
Does your school provide training on the duties and on broader issues of disability equality?			
Does your school have an accessible complaints procedure?			
Does the governing body need further training and support in order to fulfil its role?			

From *Implementing the Disability Discrimination Act in Schools and Early Years Settings* (DfES, July 2006)

Case study 5

A pupil with Tourette's syndrome is stopped from going on a school visit because he has used abusive language in class. His involuntary swearing is a rare symptom of his Tourette's syndrome. The school has a policy of banning pupils from trips and after-school activities if they swear or are abusive to staff. The reason for not allowing the pupil to go on the school visit is his use of abusive language.

1   Was there less favourable treatment, and if so, is it justified?
2   What document could the school have referred to in order to seek guidance so as not to discriminate?
3   Was there a reasonable adjustment that could have been made?
4   What if your visit was to a place where the swearing could cause considerable offence, e.g. religious institution?

Suggested answers can be found on page 73.

Reasonable adjustments and the equality duty

Under the public sector equality duty, your school is required to 'advance equality of opportunity' between pupils with disabilities and their non-disabled peers. Reasonable adjustments can often be a good way of addressing this issue.

In addition, the duty requires your school to 'foster good relations between people who share a protected characteristic and those who do not'. Making reasonable adjustments in many of the case studies in this book could have avoided any discriminatory practice and also helped to contribute to your school's public sector equality duty.

Ordinarily, the interests of other pupils regarding the reasonable adjustments required for a pupil with disabilities will be irrelevant. However, there are limited circumstances where the provision of a particular reasonable adjustment for a pupil with a disability will disadvantage other pupils. This is only relevant where the adjustment results in significant disadvantage for other pupils. In such a case, it may not be reasonable to expect the school to make the adjustment. However, in this case the school will need to justify why any reasonable adjustment will disadvantage other pupils.

Example

A pupil with a disability has a skin condition that is aggravated by heat, and his parents ask that his classroom is kept at a low temperature. However, this would mean that the other pupils in the class would be uncomfortably cold. The school would not be expected to keep the classroom at a low temperature. However, it could take other steps, such as lowering the temperature a little to a level that is still comfortable for other pupils, placing the pupil in the coldest part of the room, such as by an open window, and relaxing the school uniform policy to allow him to wear cooler and more comfortable clothing.

From the Code of Practice for Schools

There will be instances where there is a duty to make an adjustment despite some inconvenience to others. In deciding what adjustments are reasonable, you must weigh the level of inconvenience to others against the substantial disadvantage faced by the pupil with the disability.

Example

A primary school plans a school trip to a local-history museum to undertake some activities. One of the pupils in the class is deaf, and as the museum does not have a hearing loop installed she will be unable to participate in the trip. The school decides to change the trip and go to a different museum, which does have a hearing loop. Although this will cause some inconvenience to the other pupils, as the travel time to the other museum may be longer, the school decides that this is a reasonable adjustment to make given the substantial disadvantage faced by the pupil if she can't attend the trip.

From the Code of Practice for Schools

You should ensure that your school staff are instructed to act in a way that is reasonable and proportionate to the circumstances. This applies to all staff, whether paid or volunteers, including supply teachers. Communications about your school's behaviour policy should highlight the need to take appropriate account of the individual pupil's age, and any special educational needs and/or disability they might have. Headteachers should arrange training and manage information-sharing routines that ensure staff are able to fulfil this requirement.

Remember, the responsible body for your school is required to make reasonable adjustments to education and associated services so as to prevent a pupil with a disability from being excluded. The act of exclusion is a procedural step: it is what happens before that final step that is important.

Figure 2.3 Reasonable adjustments.

Examples of situations your school should avoid

The following are examples of unfortunate situations your school should avoid. They illustrate the importance of sensitivity to individual needs. Some of the inappropriate school responses described here contravene the Equality Act, and could result in the school being taken to tribunal.

Example _____

A pupil is reprimanded for failure to follow a long and complicated instruction given by an adult, but the pupil has speech and language difficulties and cannot process complex language. This is known by the school.

A more appropriate response would be for the adult to make instructions short, and clarify understanding by asking the child to repeat them.

Example _____

A pupil who has Tourette's syndrome is disciplined for making personal comments about an adult's appearance. Even though the pupil knows that such comments can be hurtful and should be avoided, his disability makes it difficult for him to control his urge to do this.

A more appropriate response would be for a staff member to tell the pupil that although the comment was hurtful and inappropriate, they understand that the child did not mean to do this. The member of staff could ask the pupil if this is indeed the case. All staff including the pupil's key worker or the SENCO should be informed about the pupil's syndrome, but not apply a sanction. The school should also ask the pupil and their family if they can give any support or advice on how to handle future situations. The pupil may like to ask the school to support him in telling his peers about his Tourette's syndrome, so a general awareness of it is known in the school.

Treating people with disabilities more favourably

It is never unlawful discrimination to treat a pupil with a disability *more* favourably than a non-disabled pupil because of their disability.

A non-disabled pupil cannot bring a claim of discrimination against the school in this case. This is called 'positive action'. It means that your school can lawfully provide additional or bespoke education, benefits, facilities or services, separate facilities, targeted resources or opportunities to benefit pupils with disabilities only, and your school can offer them on more favourable terms.

The Equality Act states that:

a. If the school thinks that a pupil with a disability is experiencing disadvantage, they can take action to enable or encourage the pupil to overcome that disadvantage.
b. If the school thinks that a pupil with a disability has needs that are different from their non-disabled peers, they can take action to meet those needs.
c. If the school thinks that participation in an activity by pupils with disabilities is disproportionately low compared with their non-disabled peers, then the school may take any proportionate action to enable or encourage them to participate in that activity.

What is proportionate?

The Act says schools may take any *proportionate* action. 'Proportionate' refers to the balancing of competing relevant factors. A balance must be struck between the seriousness of the disadvantage, the degree to which the need is different and the extent of the low participation in the particular activity, against the impact of the action on other protected groups, and the relative disadvantage, need or participation of these groups.

You should ask yourselves if the action is an appropriate way to achieve your stated aim. If so, is the proposed action reasonably necessary to achieve the aim in all of the circumstances? Would it be possible to achieve the aim as effectively by other actions that are less likely to result in less favourable treatment of others?

Example

A school has a policy of awarding a £10 voucher for those pupils with a 100 per cent attendance record. The parent of a boy with a disability complained that the boy's absences from school were due to hospital visits connected directly to his disability, and that he should be eligible to receive the voucher, as it is not his fault that he could not reach 100 per cent attendance. The parent requests that the boy be given more favourable treatment in this case.

The school replied that to allow any child to be an exception would put the school in a very difficult position in deciding who should, and what criteria would allow an absence not to be considered when awarding 100 per cent attendance. The school felt that there were simply too many cases where a parent could claim that it is not the fault of the child; for example, a child with a broken arm having to attend a fracture clinic or a child that was particularly susceptible to colds or someone that caught chickenpox.

The school voiced concerns with the parent's request for more favourable treatment for their child because they felt they would have to be extremely careful to avoid claims of positive discrimination, and therefore did not comply with the parent's request.

In this example there would seem to be a blanket policy about how the school will reward pupils for 100 per cent attendance. In this circumstance, it would be beneficial to differentiate the policy to allow children with disabilities to be treated differently. The school should take into account that pupils who meet the definition of disability would come under the protection of the EA, so it would *not* be unlawful to treat them more favourably than their non-disabled peers. This means that a school can offer benefits (in this case the voucher) to pupils with disabilities on more favourable terms, and this would be lawful.

Although taking positive action is optional, it is intended to be a measure that will allow schools to provide additional benefits to some pupils to address their disadvantage. Provided positive action is within the parameters laid down in the Act and meets the test of proportionality, it will not amount to discrimination under the Act. Remember: *it is never unlawful to treat pupils with disabilities more favourably than non-disabled pupils.*

The school's equality duty

Under the public sector equality duty, schools are required to advance equality of opportunity between pupils with disabilities and their non-disabled peers. They are also required to 'foster good relations between people who share a protected characteristic and those who do not'. Positive action can often be a legitimate way of addressing this duty.

It is common for prizes to be given to a whole class for good attendance. Without positive action, a pupil with a disability may affect the chances of the class receiving the prize. Not only could this be deemed indirect discrimination, because the child cannot achieve the aim for a reason related to their disability, but it would also obviously engender a feeling of resentment from the rest of the class toward the pupil with the disability. This would contravene the school's duty to foster good relations between people who share a protected characteristic and those who do not. Positive action in this case would avoid discrimination and contribute to the school's public sector equality duties.

Discrimination by association and perception

The new definition of direct discrimination (see page 14) also covers cases where discrimination occurs because of a victim's *association* with someone with a particular protected characteristic, e.g. a parent or another member of the family. The Act would protect people who are caring for a child with a disability. For example, an employer of the parent of a disabled child must make reasonable adjustments for them, for example, in being more flexible with start and finish times.

Protection is also provided where someone is *wrongly thought* to have a disability and is treated less favourably because of that belief, e.g. a school mistakenly believes a potential pupil to be disabled and refuses to admit them. This intended application of the direct discrimination provision represents one of the most significant expansions of protection in the Equality Act.

Harassment

Harassment occurs if you engage in unwanted behaviour that is related to a child's disability and which violates the child's dignity, or creates an intimidating, hostile, degrading, humiliating or offensive environment for the child. It is not necessary for the child to say that they object to the behaviour for it to be unwanted. It also includes situations where the pupil is *associated* with someone who has a disability, or is wrongly *perceived* as having a disability.

Unwanted conduct covers a wide range of behaviour, including spoken or written words, or abuse, imagery, graffiti, physical gestures, facial expressions, mimicry, jokes, pranks, acts affecting a pupil's surroundings, or other physical behaviour.

Example _____

A teacher makes several comments to a pupil with restricted growth about an advertisement she has seen on television depicting people of restricted growth as Christmas elves, saying how funny it would be if he participated in the school Christmas play dressed as one of Santa's helpers. The pupil finds these comments very degrading and humiliating. He does not have to protest to the teacher about them for the conduct to be unwanted and constitute harassment under the Act.

From the Code of Practice for Schools

Example

A classroom assistant starts yelling at the pupils in a class telling them to shut up and stop being such 'retards'. A pupil in the class with cerebral palsy finds these comments offensive and degrading and it is likely that it would be reasonable for this conduct to amount to harassment under the provisions of the Act.

From the Code of Practice for Schools

Victimisation

Victimisation is defined in the Act as: *Subjecting a pupil to detriment because they have done a 'protected act' (or because you believe they have done or are going to do a protected act).*

A 'protected act' is:

- making a claim of discrimination under the Act;
- helping someone else to make a claim by giving evidence or information;
- making an allegation that the school or someone else has breached the Act;
- doing anything else in connection with the Act.

'Detriment' is not defined in the Act and could take many forms. Generally, a detriment is anything the pupil concerned might reasonably consider changed their position for the worse or put them at a disadvantage. This might include:

- being excluded;
- being given lower marks;
- disciplinary action;
- being denied opportunities.

However, an unjustified sense of grievance would not be considered a detriment.

School pupils who are victimised because a family member has carried out a protected act are also protected under the Act. If your school or a member of staff treats a child less favourably because they have taken such action, then this will be unlawful victimisation. There must be a link between what the child or their associate did and your treatment of them. The less favourable treatment does not need to be linked to their disability for victimisation to have occurred. Ex-pupils are also covered by victimisation rules.

Example

A parent of a child with a disability has complained about bullying at school experienced by her child and the lack of sufficient action taken by the school to deal with it effectively. The same school then refuses to allow the parent to hire its sports facilities, which are available to the general public, believing the parent, because of the previous complaints, will only attempt to find further fault with the school's policies, practices or facilities. This would constitute unlawful victimisation.

From the Code of Practice for Schools

Example _____

A parent claims her child has been subjected to disability discrimination when the school doesn't provide her child with her first choice of work experience placement. She loses the case as the tribunal accepts the school's explanation that the placement was not provided for her child because of a valid reason unconnected to the child's disability. At a parents' meeting after this ruling she again asserts that her child was not provided with the work experience placement she requested due to disability discrimination.

She is upset when people point out that she lost her case and the matter is over. Her grievance does not constitute a detriment and this response is not victimisation.

From the Code of Practice for Schools

Promoting positive attitudes towards people with disabilities

The most prevalent form of harassment to pupils with disabilities in schools is bullying by other pupils. Improving schools' attitudes towards bullying will help address the high number of pupils with disabilities that are currently being bullied in our schools. It is estimated that children with disabilities are ten times more likely to be victims of bullying than non-disabled children.

It will help your school's efforts to reduce bullying by working in partnership with other agencies to implement strategies to address the problem. To promote effective interventions, the entire school community must be involved, rather than focusing on the perpetrators and victims alone.

To change 'hearts and minds', schools should help pupils feel more comfortable about talking to and interacting with SEN and disabled children. The way school staff react to disability and inclusion will greatly affect how pupils react. Since it is teachers that generally set the example for their classes, their response pattern will prompt similar responses in their pupils, so there is a great deal that teachers and other school staff can do to promote disability in a positive light. For example:

- positive literature and images of disability (appropriate for key stage);
- investigating people in history with a disability;
- guest speakers (achievers with disabilities);
- peer training;
- whole-school training (including lunchtime staff and parent support);
- staff modelling respectful attitudes towards pupils with disabilities, staff and parents;
- ensuring representation of people with disabilities in senior positions in the school;
- positive images in school books and other materials;
- pupils with disabilities on the school council.

Promoting positive attitudes and actions will help with the implementation of your equality duty.

Additional resources

These booklets can be found on the Inclusive Choice website:

- Code of Practice for Schools
- Code of Practice for Services, Public Functions and Associations
- Draft Code of Practice for Schools
- Duties and Definitions
- Early Years and the Disability Discrimination Act
- Equality Act (2010) – What Do I Need to Know – Disability Quick Start Guide
- Extending Inclusion
- Inclusion – Providing Effective Learning Opportunities for all Pupils
- Making Reasonable Adjustments for Disabled Pupils
- Reasonable Adjustments and the DDA
- SEN Code of Practice
- What Equality Law Means for You as an Education Provider – Schools
- What Equality Law Means for Your Association, Club or Society

3 How the law affects school life

Figure 3.1 Equality of aspiration.

The Equality Duty is only briefly described in this book. It is a large subject and requires its own book, which is available from Inclusive Choice at www.inclusivechoice.com.

In 2005, the Disability Equality Duty (DED) legislation came into force as part 5A of the Disability Discrimination Act. This legislation has now been subsumed into the Equality Act, 2010. The DED is meant to ensure that all public bodies – such as central or local government, schools, health trusts or emergency services – pay 'due regard' to the promotion of equality for people with disabilities in every area of their work. All schools maintained by a local authority and academies are subject to the public sector equality duty. Part of the school's duty under the DDA was to write a Disability Equality Scheme. Although this is no longer a requirement under the Equality Act, there are still documents that must be published, which amount to a very similar set of information that was required to be in your DES.

Previously, there were three separate equality duties – disability, race and gender. You may wish to combine these three into a single one (a single equality duty), or you may leave the three separate. Almost all the requirements of the original Disability Equality Duty are still present in the new equality duty, although there have been some changes of names.

The equality duty includes two elements – a general duty and a specific duty. Both apply to all publicly funded schools, and responsibility for the duty lies with the governing body. The EHRC can take action against schools that have not met their duties.

The Equality Act introduces a Single Equality Duty, which applies to all protected characteristics. Key dates for the equality duty are:

5 April 2011	General and specific duties come into force.
31 July 2011	Organisations (except schools) to publish equality information.
31 December 2011	Schools to publish equality information.
6 April 2012	Organisations (including schools) to publish equality objectives.

The duties require schools to take steps not just to eliminate unlawful discrimination and harassment but also to actively promote equality. This is very similar to what your school will already be doing under its present Disability Equality Duty.

The general duty

The general duty requires schools, when carrying out their functions, to have due regard to the need to:

- eliminate discrimination, harassment and victimisation;
- advance equality of opportunity between people with disabilities and non-disabled people;
- foster good relations between disabled people and non-disabled people.

These are called the *three aims* of the Equality Duty. They replace the six elements of the old Disability Equality Duty. However, in practice, very little has changed, because the old six elements are all included in these three aims (Figure 3.2).

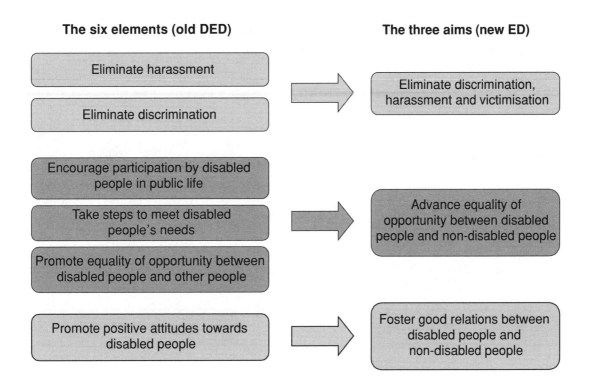

Figure 3.2 How names have changed in the equality duty.

The three aims apply across schools' duties to all pupils, staff, parents, and users of the school with disabilities. It does not bring in new rights for people with disabilities, but it does require schools to take a more proactive approach to promoting disability equality and eliminating discrimination.

The specific duty

The specific duty requires your school to demonstrate how you are meeting the general duty. In effect, the general duty sets out *what* you have to do and the specific duty sets out *how* you have to do it, and what you need to record as evidence of what you have done.

You are required to undertake the development of your equality duty documents in a particular way and to include particular elements. You must engage with pupils and parents with disabilities in the preparation of these documents; they should not just be a description of what you and your school want to do. Only children and parents with disabilities (and to a certain extent staff) who use the school know what really matters to them. You must describe in your documents how you have engaged with people with disabilities and involved them.

In addition, your documents must set out your arrangements for gathering information on the effect your school's policies have on:

● the educational opportunities available to and the achievements of pupils with disabilities;
● your methods for assessing the impact of your current or proposed policies and practices on disability equality;
● the steps you are going to take to meet the general duty (the school's action plan);
● the arrangements for using information to support the review of the action plan in the future.

The Disability Equality Duty had three *specific duties*. These have been renamed from the DED to focus work on the most important matters.

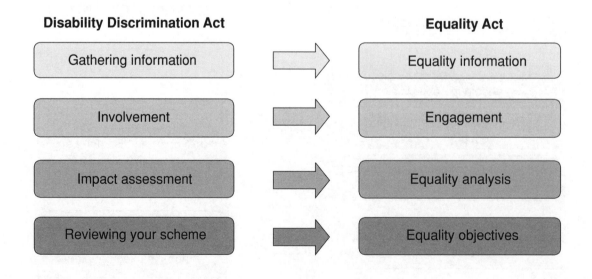

Figure 3.3 How names have changed in the equality duty.

The requirements to regularly review your scheme and make action plans to improve it have been termed *Equality objectives*. After you have set your equality objectives, you will be expected to publish information that enables both you and the public to measure how successful you have been in meeting them. You are expected to do this at least annually.

Your school is not required to do anything under the equality duty that is unreasonable or impracticable. If you are already making reasonable adjustments at a whole-school level and have a well-developed accessibility plan, you may find that you are well on the way to meeting your equality duty.

Relevance

The General Equality Duty applies to public authorities, including schools, whatever their size. The way in which it is implemented, however, should be appropriate to the size and nature of its functions. For a school, this means everything that you are *required* to do as well as everything that you are *allowed* to do. Teaching of pupils is obviously the primary service, but the duty also covers policies and procedures, budgetary decisions, allocating resources, regulation, employment of staff, audits and inspections, external communication, commissioning services, procuring goods, partnerships, management of premises, etc.

For a school, certain protected characteristics will obviously be more relevant than others, and certain functions of the school are more relevant than others. This should be reflected in the work that you do and the information that you publish.

What needs to be published?

Although there is no longer a requirement to develop and publish a Disability Equality Scheme, you may wish to present your objectives within a similar document, if that has been an effective approach for organising your equality information and for communicating your plans to stakeholders. Therefore, your existing DES can become the basis of your new published information.

You must meet all the other publication requirements, which are detailed below.

Compliance with the General Equality Duty

You must publish sufficient information to demonstrate your compliance with the General Equality Duty (the three aims). This must be done by 31 December 2011, and at least annually after that, from the first date of publication.

This must include:

- the effect of your policies and practices on children with protected characteristics in accordance with the three aims;
- the analysis you have undertaken to establish whether the policies and practices have furthered the three aims;
- details of the information you considered in carrying out this analysis;
- details of the engagement you undertook.

Equality objectives

You must publish your equality objectives by 5 April 2012 and every four years after that. This should include:

- objectives you intend to achieve to meet one or more aims of the general equality duty;
- details of the engagement that you undertook in developing these objectives.

The objectives should be specific and measurable, and should set out how progress will be measured.

The Equality and Human Rights Commission would normally expect to see the information published broken down by protected group. It would usually include:

- performance information; for example, pupil attainment;
- access to services (lessons, school trips etc. and reasonable adjustments put in place);
- satisfaction with services;
- complaints from parents, with an indication of reasons for complaints.

Preparing for the work

You may find it helpful to appoint a working group of three or four people to steer the development and to report to the governing body. For example:

- a **senior manager** – the scope is across the school's responsibilities, so at least one member of the group needs to be a senior manager in order to draw on links with every area of the school's work;
- a **person with a disability** – a member of staff with a disability or a pupil with a disability. Throughout the process, the group will need to review the extent to which they are hearing the views of a range of pupils, staff and parents, with a range of impairments;
- **other members** – it may be helpful to incorporate a range of perspectives into the group by recruiting across curriculum and pastoral responsibilities, across length of service in the school and across teaching and non-teaching responsibilities.

References

A full book about the Equality Duty, which complements this book, is available from Inclusive Choice at www.inclusivechoice.com.

There is a set of five booklets published by the Equality and Human Rights Commission that explain the new duty in detail. They can be downloaded free from the EHRC website (www.equalityhumanrights.com). The documents are:

1   The Essential Guide to the Public Sector Equality Duty
2   Equality Analysis and the Equality Duty: A Guide for Public Authorities
3   Engagement and the Equality Duty: A Guide for Public Authorities
4   Equality Objectives and the Equality Duty: A Guide for Public Authorities
5   Equality Information and the Equality Duty. A Guide for Public Authorities

Admissions

Under the Equality Act, admission arrangements and other policies must be fair and must not unfairly disadvantage, either directly or indirectly, a child with a disability or special educational needs. You should develop and implement admission arrangements, practices and over-subscription criteria that actively promote equality, and thus go further than simply ensuring that unfair practices and criteria are excluded. Remember, it is never unlawful discrimination to treat a pupil with a disability *more* favourably than a non-disabled pupil because of their disability.

You must not discriminate against prospective pupils with disabilities in their access to education. Three distinct aspects of admission are specifically covered. You must not discriminate against a child with a disability:

a. in the arrangements you make for determining pupil admission to the school;
b. in the terms on which you offer to admit a child with a disability to the school;
c. by refusing or deliberately omitting to accept an application for admission.

Instances when it may not be possible to include specific children

Children who have special educational needs but do not have statements must be educated in mainstream schools apart from in exceptional circumstances. The Code of Practice on School Admissions states that admission authorities should not make subjective judgements. If a pupil, once admitted, is found to be seriously and persistently disruptive, then the school may consider disciplinary action, including temporary or permanent exclusion. It is also unacceptable for a school to refuse to admit a child thought to be *potentially* disruptive or to exhibit challenging behaviour on the grounds that the child ought first to be assessed for special educational needs.

The Equality Act says that it is unlawful for the responsible body of a school to discriminate against or victimise a person:

a. in the arrangements it makes for deciding who is offered admission as a pupil;
b. as to the terms on which it offers to admit the person as a pupil;
c. by not admitting the person as a pupil.

Academies

Some, but not all, academies are required to comply with the Admission Code; however irrespective of the contents of the funding agreement, academies must comply with the Equality Act and the guidance in this code.

Bad practice in admissions

The following example is a real case of a school SENCO. It is taken from a report published in December 2006 by the National Children's Bureau.

Example ———————————————————————————————————————

'What I've done is I've invited parents in, sometimes with the child, sometimes without the child, and I have walked them around the building. Quite fast, sometimes quite deliberately when there's a lot of movement going on and then I've just turned to the parent and said, 'Do you think your child could cope with this?' So rather than say, "no",' I would say to the parent, 'Do you think this is fair?' I think sometimes you have to let parents realise for themselves that this just isn't an appropriate placement.'

Most people in this day and age know not to discriminate directly. However, they still make errors like this SENCO.

Actions such as these could result in the school finding itself in a tribunal for indirect discrimination. The question the SENCO could have asked themselves in this case is 'What reasonable adjustment could our school make?' This SENCO is seeing the prospective pupil as the problem – pursuing reasons why the child *can't* be admitted. If the parents were to bring about a complaint of discrimination, the school would need to consider whether there is any justification for the SENCO's practice.

Example ———————————————————————————————————————

A pupil seeking admission who has Tourette's syndrome is being interviewed for a place at a school. He makes inappropriate comments during the interview, and for this reason is not selected for admission. The fact that the school didn't know that the prospective pupil has Tourette's syndrome may not be a defence, because no attempt is made by the school to establish if there was a particular reason for this behaviour. This could constitute unlawful discrimination arising from disability, unless it can be objectively justified.

From the Code of Practice for Schools

In the previous example, it would seem that the school relies on their behaviour policy to determine whether or not the school will admit a pupil who has made inappropriate comments. The school seems to have a 'blanket policy' on expected behaviour of a pupil and this may be why they have made their decision not to admit the pupil. In a case such as this, a parent would be advised to remind school of its duties to pupils with disabilities and also to ask the school if it has a differentiated policy in relation to pupils with disabilities and behavioural needs.

The Act envisages that schools will adopt an approach of 'What can we do to ensure that this child *is* included?' Other examples of good practice are:

● The school should be aware of their *anticipatory* duty to make reasonable adjustments for pupils with disabilities.
● Review the school's practice of how they show prospective pupils with disabilities and their families around the school.
● Make sure prospective pupils and families feel that the school is interested in talking about 'reasonable adjustments' and that it actively seeks and welcomes any opinions and advice offered by pupils and their families.
● In a large school, where a variety of people may show prospective students around, it is important that everyone realises the implications of seemingly innocent actions and comments (as above). It is good practice to ensure all staff are trained in the school's disability discrimination duties.

The example above shows why it is important for parents to disclose their children's disabilities in order for the school to be anticipatory and make reasonable adjustments.

Exclusions

It is only pupils with disabilities and potential pupils with disabilities who are covered by the duties in the Act. It will be for the SEN and Disability Tribunal and admissions and exclusions appeals panels in England and Wales, and for the Sheriff Court in Scotland, to determine whether or not a child has a disability for the purposes of the Act.

The duties make it unlawful for a responsible body to discriminate against a pupil with a disability by excluding him or her from the school for a reason related to their disability. This would be less favourable treatment. The duties apply to exclusions whether they are:

- in Scotland, temporary exclusions or exclusion/removal from register;
- in England and Wales, permanent or fixed-term exclusions.

Learning support units or short-term use of pupil referral units can also play a significant part in ensuring that pupils are able to remain in mainstream education, or make a successful return following exclusion. Schools and local education authorities need to share good practice in supporting pupils who present challenging and disruptive behaviour. Schools can draw on the expertise of special schools – particularly those who cater for pupils with emotional and behavioural problems – and pupil referral units.

It is important to know that when your school is involved in the exclusion of a child with a disability, you must have clear evidence of any action you have taken in order to avoid the exclusion. The example below which we've seen earlier shows how one school was able to provide a detailed report of why an exclusion had taken place, and was thereby cleared of a charge of discrimination.

Example

A child attending his local mainstream school has speech and language difficulties and exhibits challenging behaviour. Throughout his schooling he has been inclined to kick and lash out, turn over tables and chairs, damage work and throw objects scissors on one occasion. Other pupils have to be kept out of the way and on at least one occasion his class teacher has been scratched and kicked by him. His behaviour book records some incidents where he has hurt other children and himself. The school felt it had no alterative but to temporarily exclude the child.

The child's parent has claimed that the school unlawfully discriminated against their son with regards to less favourable treatment and claimed that no reasonable adjustments were made in order to ensure the exclusion did not take place. Therefore, the parent has referred their case to the SEND tribunal.

A tribunal would have to consider the parent's claim of less favourable treatment, then ask what the school did to avoid treating the child less favourably and what reasonable adjustments were undertaken by the school.

In this case the school was able to produce reports on advice received, and input from the local authority's behavioural support service since the child's admission to the school. Other professionals had also contributed to his programmes, including an educational psychologist and the local authority's behavioural and specialist SEN support services. The important point here is that the school was able to show the tribunal a document trail of extra support.

The school was also able to show detailed behavioural management techniques utilised, programmes including reward systems that had been effective, and efforts to encourage continuation of these techniques at home.

The headteacher and the experienced learning support assistant gave details of the provision put in place for the child by the school and his progress since he arrived. They mentioned procedures that they followed and agencies and persons from whom they took advice. The school produced copies of the home–school liaison material to show how they had worked to build up good relationships with home.

The tribunal concluded that the school took into account the child's needs and disabilities and made reasonable adjustments to avoid putting him at a substantial disadvantage so that he was not treated less favourably than others without a disability.

In this case the tribunal found that the school did not unlawfully discriminate against the child, and therefore ruled in favour of the school. This is mainly because it was clear that the school had a well-documented account of all the reasonable adjustments it had put in place and of the outside agencies it had worked in partnership with in order to provide best practices for the child.

Even though in this case the school won the tribunal case, it would still be advisable for the school to consider if their relationship with the parent could have been better, what they would do differently and if any policy or practice could do with reviewing?

Academies

Some, but not all, academies are required by their funding agreement to follow the exclusions guidance. However, irrespective of the contents of the funding agreement, academies must comply with the Equality Act and the guidance in this code.

Transport

Although transport to school for children with disabilities is not under the control of your school, it is useful for you to know about it so that you can advise parents. Parents are generally unaware of their rights, and so often simply accept the decision of the local authority in this respect. A disrupted, overlong or late journey to school can make a child's school day start badly, which may impact on their performance and behaviour during the school day. Therefore, it is important for the school as well as the child that this journey is as efficient and timely as possible. It is therefore in your interests as a school to help parents of your pupils with disabilities to get good transport to school.

Pupils with disabilities will not thrive in every school. Unfortunately, not all schools are as inclusive as yours may be. Therefore, it is common that pupils with disabilities may have to travel further to school, and quite possible that their disability precludes them from walking as other children might. That is why the Education and Inspections Act 2006 inserted new school transport provisions into the Education Act 1996. It places a duty on local authorities in England to make suitable travel arrangements free of charge for eligible children, as they consider necessary, to facilitate their attendance at school.

Who it applies to – 'eligible children'

The local authority's duty to provide transport applies to children up to sixth-form age to:

- all those resident in the authority's area, and receiving education or training; and
- those not resident in the authority's area, but who travel within it to receive education or training.

Children who are eligible for school transport are referred to as 'eligible children'. Some children with SEN or a disability may be unable to walk even relatively short distances to school, and this makes them eligible children. This means that local authorities must make suitable travel arrangements for them.

> ### Example
> Lilly is a five-year-old child with cerebral palsy, which severely restricts her mobility. Her parents receive higher-level disability living allowance (DLA) in recognition of this. Lilly attends her nearest suitable school, which is one mile from her home. Receipt of higher-level DLA indicates that it would not be reasonable to expect her to walk to school and so she is eligible for free transport.

> ### Example
> Darren is 12 years old and has an autistic spectrum disorder. He attends his nearest suitable school which is two-and-a-half miles from his home. He is unaware of danger and has to be accompanied even on very short journeys. Darren's doctor has confirmed that, in her opinion, his carer is unable to prevent Darren from being exposed to the risks arising from his lack of awareness of danger for a journey of this length. To comply with their duty, the local authority must ensure that suitable arrangements for Darren are in place.

However, just because the child has a disability or SEN, whether statemented or not, does not mean that the local authority must provide transport for them. If the child's disability does not stop them from walking to school (and the school is within two miles if they are under 8, or three miles otherwise) or make it unsafe for them to do so, then the local authority are within their rights not to provide free transport.

Selection of school

The parents' preferred school might be further away from the child's home than another school that can also meet the child's special educational needs. In such a case, it might be open to the local authority to name the nearer school if that would be compatible with the efficient use of the local authority's resources. It would also be open to the local authority to name the school preferred by the child's parents on condition that the parents agree to meet all or part of the transport costs.

Transport in statements of SEN

If the child has a statement of SEN, which has transport requirements written into it, the local authority must provide them. Transport is normally only recorded in the statement in part 6 in exceptional cases where the child has particular transport needs. In most cases local authorities will have clear general policies relating to transport for children with SEN that should be made available to parents and schools.

What journeys does it cover?

The duty covers journeys to and from school at the start and end of the day, and also includes attendance at before- and after-school activities.

Suitability of arrangements

For a local authority to meet their legal requirements, travel arrangements must be suitable. The suitability of arrangements will depend on a number of factors:

- The arrangements must enable the child to reach school without such stress, strain or difficulty that they would be prevented from benefiting from the education provided. In a court case in 1992, the court decided that the transport provided by the local authority must be 'non-stressful' if the child was to benefit from education.
- The arrangements must allow the child to travel in reasonable safety and in reasonable comfort.
- The journey time must be reasonable. The time will depend on a number of factors, including the age and any individual needs of the child. The maximum length of journey for a child of primary-school age should be 45 minutes, and for a secondary-school child should be up to 75 minutes each way. A child's disability might be such that a shorter journey time is appropriate.
- Although the service needn't be a door-to-door service, children are not expected to walk an unreasonably long distance to catch a public service bus, or a bus journey that ends an unreasonably long distance from the school.

Arrangements could not be considered to be suitable where, for example, the child must make several changes of public service bus to get to school, which results in an unreasonably long journey time.

Government guidance advises on particular issues affecting pupils with severe learning difficulties and it recommends that local authorities:

- ensure that drivers and escorts are known to parents;
- operator contact numbers are provided for parents;
- ensure stability of staffing arrangements for pupils who dislike change;
- encourage schools and transport services to use a home–school liaison diary;
- ensure that journey times are reasonable to avoid undue stress.

Drivers and escorts

Transport for pupils with disabilities should be provided by drivers and escorts who have enhanced CRB checks. Local authorities should ensure that all drivers and escorts have undertaken disability equality training. It is also good practice for those responsible for planning and managing school transport to have disability equality training. This training must consist of:

- an awareness of different types of disability including hidden disabilities;
- an awareness of what constitutes discrimination;
- training in the necessary skills to recognise, support and manage pupils with different types of disabilities, including hidden disabilities and certain behaviour that may be associated with such disabilities;
- training in the skills necessary to communicate appropriately with pupils with all types of disabilities, including hidden disabilities; and
- training in the implementation of healthcare protocols to cover emergency procedures.

Parents with disabilities

The Equality Act places a duty on local authorities to promote equality of opportunity for people with disabilities and to eliminate discrimination. This duty is anticipatory, meaning that local authorities must review all their policies, practices, procedures and services to make sure they do not discriminate against people with disabilities, and to ensure that all their services are planned with the needs of people with disabilities fully considered in advance.

This means that local authorities will be under a duty to amend their home-to-school transport policy if, for example, that policy relied on parents with disabilities accompanying their non-disabled children along a walking route for it to be considered safe for the child, and where the parents' disability prevented them from doing so. In such circumstances, a reasonable adjustment would be for the local authority to provide free home-to-school transport for the children of parents with disabilities.

Complaints and appeals

Before complaining, it is good to be armed with as much information as possible. The law requires local authorities to publish their policies relating to school travel. Knowing the local authority's own policies is invaluable if you know they are not adhering to them. The local authority must consult widely on any changes to their policies on school travel arrangements, with all interested parties included in the consultations. Consultations should last for at least 28 working days during term time. This period should be extended to take account of any school holidays that may occur during the period of consultation. Any such changes should be phased in and come into effect as pupils start school. If the local authority has not done this, or parents have not had any opportunity to comment, this will strengthen their position in any complaint.

Local authorities should have in place a robust appeals procedure for parents to follow should they have cause for complaint or disagreement concerning the eligibility of their child for travel support. The details of appeals procedures should be published alongside travel policy statements. Each local authority may have a different appeals process, so parents should contact their local authority, or find the process on their website, before starting their appeal.

If the parent is unhappy with the way their appeal is dealt with, they can complain to the local government ombudsman. Sometimes complaints and appeals may be made to the secretary of state or the high court. The ombudsman considers the way a decision is reached, not with the merits of the decision itself, so parents cannot complain just because they do not agree with a decision. The main test of whether there has been maladministration is whether an authority has acted reasonably within the law, its own policies and the good practice standards of local administration. The ombudsman expects complaints to be made to the local authority first before they will investigate.

The local government ombudsman website can be found at http://www.lgo.org.uk.

Bad timekeeping

The transport service provided should ensure that the child arrives in good time for the school day. Equally, the child should not be expected to leave any earlier than other children at the end of the school day (although a child may leave a few minutes early for safety reasons to avoid the end-of-day rush).

The local authority's disability equality duty requires them to ensure that they do not discriminate against people with disabilities, and that all their services are planned with the needs of people with disabilities fully considered in advance. In addition, the Equality Act says that they must not provide less favourable treatment to a child with a disability for a reason related to their disability. In practice, this means that they must ensure that the transport arrangements do not place the child at any disadvantage over non-disabled children. If the child arrives late or is forced to leave early, this clearly places them at a disadvantage.

Example

A school has closed its entrance barrier, preventing a pupil who is a wheelchair user from accessing the designated disabled parking bay by the school's main entrance when he leaves his school. The pupil now has to access his taxi away from the school entrance via an uneven footpath which is proving to be difficult and danger-ous, and has caused damaged to his electric wheelchair. If his taxi is late, the pupil has to wait outside in the rain or cold.

The school's reason for closing the barrier is to safeguard non-disabled pupils who they say may be in danger as the taxi drives to the disabled bay.

The school has said that to avoid this danger, the pupil must leave school 15 minutes early or 15 minutes late when the flow of other pupils has diminished.

The school's actions may constitute discrimination on the grounds of less favourable treatment toward the pupil with a disability, and the pupil being placed at a substantial disadvantage.

To decide whether a school has treated a pupil 'less favourably', a comparison must be made with how it would have treated other non-disabled pupils in similar circumstances. If the school's treatment of the pupil with a disability puts them at a clear disadvantage compared with other pupils, it is likely that the treatment will be less favourable. Non-disabled pupils are not required to leave 15 minutes early or late. If the quality of the education, benefit, facility or service being offered, or the manner in which it is offered, is comparatively poor, this could also amount to less favourable treatment. If the pupil is leaving school considerably earlier than other pupils, and this is for a reason related to their disability, it could be considered that the pupil is being placed at a substantial disadvantage.

What reasonable adjustments could have been made?

- The school could have considered adding signs to inform wheelchair users which pathway to use.
- The school should have monitored the physical condition of the pathways they intended the pupil to use, to ensure it was not dangerous for him.
- The school could have implemented a buddy system to help access to the school for vulnerable pupils and pupils with disabilities.
- The barrier could have been manned for the few minutes that it would have taken for the taxi to leave the premises.
- Keep parents informed of any changes you intend to implement that may affect their child.

Managing medicines

Under the Equality Act, responsible bodies for schools (including nursery schools) must not discriminate against pupils with disabilities in relation to their access to education and associated services – a broad term that covers all aspects of school life including school trips, school clubs and activities.

Your school should be making reasonable adjustments for children with disabilities, including those with medical needs, in your practices, procedures and policies. Health and safety issues must not be used spuriously to avoid making reasonable adjustments. You should avoid making uninformed assumptions about health and safety risks.

Example

A pupil with a stair-climbing wheelchair applies to a large secondary school with several flights of stairs. The school prevents the child from using the stair-climbing wheelchair in the school as they think it will be dangerous. However, after carrying out a risk assessment and finding out more about the wheelchair, the school realises that it doesn't present a significant health and safety risk and therefore it would be reasonable to allow the child to use it.

From the Code of Practice for Schools

Parents have the prime responsibility for their child's health and should provide their child's school with information about their child's medical condition. Parents are a valuable resource when including children with disabilities, as they are often the ones that know best how to deal with issues concerning their child, and they may be implementing useful practices at home.

There is no legal duty that requires school staff to administer medicines. A number of schools are developing roles for support staff that build the administration of medicines into their core job description. Some support staff may have such a role in their contract of employment. Your school should ensure that you have sufficient members of support staff who are appropriately trained to manage medicines as part of their duties.

Positive responses by your school to a child's medical needs will not only benefit the child directly but can also positively influence the attitude of their peers and promote positive images of disability, which is a requirement of your equality duty.

Example _____

A child has a condition where the school is required to administer emergency medication in the form of an injection. Staff at the school have raised concerns about administering the injection as it involves quite a complicated procedure. The school contacts the child's mother and asks her opinion on the matter and whether they have another way of doing this. The parent, in turn, contacts the hospital and arrangements are made for a nurse to come to the school and talk through their concerns. The parent is invited along also.

Training and insurance

Staff who administer medicines should receive appropriate training and support from health professionals. Where employers' policies are that schools should manage medicines, there should be robust systems in place to ensure that medicines are managed safely. There must be an assessment of the risks to the health and safety of staff and others, and measures put in place to manage any identified risks.

Staff who volunteer to administer medicines should be indemnified by the education authority's insurance policy. In addition, the education authority should likewise indemnify any member of staff acting in good faith for the benefit of a pupil in an emergency situation.

Medical needs of non-SEN children

A medical diagnosis or a disability does not necessarily imply SEN. It may not be necessary for a child or young person with any particular diagnosis or medical condition to have a statement, or to need any form of additional educational provision. It is the child's educational needs rather than a medical diagnosis that must be considered. Some pupils may not require statements or school-based SEN provision but they have medical conditions that, if not properly managed, could hinder their access.

Children with medical needs do not necessarily have SEN. For example, those with severe asthma, severe eczema, diabetes, epilepsy, childhood cancer and a range of other conditions.

School trips

The Equality Act makes it is unlawful to discriminate against pupils with disabilities in the education or associated services provided for pupils at school. This includes after-school activities such as sporting clubs, drama and musical productions, whether educational or not, and whether or not they are organised and run by the school. The range of activities, and the way in which they are offered, must not unlawfully discriminate.

No distinction is made in the legislation between a school trip in term time and a school trip outside of term time. The Equality Act applies equally to both. A potential tribunal case could be considered if it was shown that the school failed in its duties not to treat pupils with disabilities less favourably and failed to make reasonable adjustments. The question will be whether there is any justification for any less favourable treatment.

Figure 3.4 School trips.

When looking to the question of any reasonable adjustments, the Act states that a school discriminates against a child with a disability if it fails to make any reasonable adjustments to the detriment of the child and without justification. Remember that the duty to make reasonable adjustments is anticipatory. A school must demonstrate that it has taken all reasonable steps and implemented any relevant reasonable adjustments necessary to ensure that off-site visits are accessible to all pupils with disabilities. Schools must not exclude a child from any associated educational activity because of their disability.

Failing to make reasonable adjustments can only be justified if there is a reason that is both *substantial* and *material* to the circumstances of the particular case. For the reason to be *material*, there has to be a clear connection between the reason the school gives and the circumstances of the particular case. The reason also has to be *substantial*, which is defined as 'more than minor or trivial'. Factors that will need to be considered, as they may give rise to a defence by the school of justification include:

- time and effort that would need to be expended;
- the inconvenience, indignity or discomfort a child with a disability might suffer;
- the loss of opportunity or the diminished progress that a child with a disability may make in comparison with their peers.

The Department for Education provides guidance on the safe conduct of school trips. This guidance emphasises the need to:

- ensure the inclusion of all pupils: *Every effort should be made to ensure that school journeys and activities are available and accessible to all who wish to participate...*;
- ensure that suitable arrangements have been put in place to ensure their safety: *The group leader should discuss the visit with the parents of pupils with SEN to ensure that suitable arrangements have been put in place to ensure their safety.*

Of course, health and safety considerations are an important part of the planning of any school trip, but they should not bar pupils with disabilities from participating. A risk assessment needs to be carried out for any school trip, and reasonable adjustments for pupils with disabilities should be part of the risk assessment. Failing to make reasonable adjustments may amount to discrimination.

Here are some examples of common objections that teachers may have to taking children with disabilities on school trips, and explanations of how the Equality Act covers them.

'I'm not in my role of a teacher on this trip, so I can do what I like.'

Although teachers on a trip may have volunteered their time, they are clearly acting in their capacity as a member of staff for the school, so cannot claim that any discriminatory decisions they make personally on the trip are not covered by the Equality Act.

'We're a grammar school and are exempt from less favourable treatment.'

Different forms of selection are permitted in different schools. For example, specialist schools can give priority in their admissions criteria to a proportion of pupils who show a particular aptitude for the subject in which the school specialises. However, these permitted criteria are concerned with school admissions, not school trips. Any selection criterion for a trip that treats a child with a disability less favourably due to their disability could well be discrimination. As an example, using a criterion based upon attendance may be discriminatory against a child who, due to their disability, was often absent.

'The school trip isn't educational anyway.'

It is possible that the loss of opportunity to go on certain trips would not diminish a child's educational progress, so much so that the child is at a substantial disadvantage when compared with their peers. As such, less favourable treatment may be justified. However, this would be dependent on the particular circumstances of the case.

'We didn't know the resort wouldn't be inclusive.'

The school is under a duty to make reasonable adjustments and these must be anticipatory. The school is expected to determine in advance whether a particular location is suitable for any children with disabilities they are taking. Again, to be justified, material and substantial, factors of a particular case would need to be looked at. If the resort chosen by the school failed to provide facilities for children with disabilities, this may well be found to be a breach of duty to provide reasonable adjustments. The failure by a school to make reasonable adjustments would be dependent on a child's individual circumstances.

It could also be treated as less favourable treatment if a child with a disability could not get their application to go on a school trip in at the same time as the other pupils because it was unclear if the transport, resort or equipment could provide for the child's particular circumstances.

Case study 6

A school is planning a skiing trip for all pupils in year 8. One of the pupils is a wheelchair user and would need support when using skis. The school informs the pupil's parents that they cannot take him because they don't have enough staff to offer support for him on the trip.

1   Since the less favourable treatment is not on the school premises, can it be justified?
2   Since the trip is outside of school hours, do the teachers still need to follow the EA, as they are then 'private citizens'?

3   If the school is a selective school, can they select pupils for the skiing trip based on aptitude, since there are a limited number of places available?
4   Could the school claim that the skiing trip is not part of the curriculum and therefore that missing it would not be detrimental to the pupil's education?
5   If the facilities at the chosen resort are not suitable for a child with a disability, would the school still be in breach of the EA?

Suggested answers can be found on page 74.

Example

A child with ADHD has broken the behaviour policy of his school. As a punishment, and because the school was worried about his future behaviour, he was excluded from class swimming lessons for several weeks. He was also not allowed to attend an after-school club. In the spring term, his class went on a school trip and he was not allowed to attend.

The child's mother made a claim to the Special Educational Needs and Disability (SEND) Tribunal that the school had discriminated against her child by treating him less favourably for a reason related to his disability and by failing to make reasonable adjustments to enable him to be included in lessons and activities alongside his non-disabled peers.

The tribunal found that the school had discriminated against the child and that the failure of the school to include disability as an aspect to be considered in their behaviour policy was a significant contributory factor. The school was ordered to:

●   include the decision in any records kept by them in relation to the child;
●   amend any records referring to the exclusions to include a statement that these were found to constitute unlawful discrimination under the Equality Act;
●   apologise to the child;
●   carry out appropriate training for staff involved in the decisions;
●   review the school's behaviour policy to ensure that it complies with the requirements of the Equality Act and the Code of Practice for Schools.

Case study 7

A pupil with cerebral palsy who uses a wheelchair is on a trip with her class to an outdoor activity centre. The teachers arrange to take the class on a 12-mile hike over difficult terrain but, having carried out a risk assessment, they decide that the pupil who uses a wheelchair will be unable to accompany her class, for health and safety reasons.

●   Is the less favourable treatment for a reason that is related to the pupil's disability?
●   Is it justified?

From the Code of Practice for Schools

Suggested answers can be found on page 75.

Additional resources

These booklets can be found on the Inclusive Choice website: www.inclusivechoice.com

- A Guide to the Law for School Governors
- A Parents' Guide to School Exclusion Appeals
- A Note of Good Practice on Unofficial Exclusion
- Back on Track
- Code of Practice for Schools
- DDA Part 5A – The Disability Equality Duty
- Duties and Definitions
- Exclusion Appeal Flowchart
- Extending Inclusion
- Fixed Period Exclusion – A Practical Guide to Parents' Legal Rights
- Flowchart for Fixed Term Exclusion
- From Exclusion to Inclusion
- Good Practice before Considering Exclusion Flowchart
- Guidance on the Disability Equality Duty
- HIV in Schools – Good Practice Guide to Supporting Children Infected or affected by HIV
- Having a Say – A Young Person's Guide to Exclusion
- Improving Access for Disabled Pupils – School Plans
- Improving Behaviour and Attendance – Guidance on Exclusion for Schools
- Including Me – Managing Complex Health Needs in Schools and Early Years Settings
- Inclusion – Providing Effective Learning Opportunities for all Pupils
- Inclusive Schooling – Children with Special Educational Needs
- Managing Medicines in Schools and Early Years Settings – Unison
- Managing Medicines in Schools and Early Years Settings – DoH
- Permanent Exclusion – A Practical Guide to Parents' Legal Rights
- Permanent Exclusion Flowchart
- School Admission Appeals Code
- School Admissions Code of Practice
- School Discipline – Your Powers and Rights as a Teacher
- School Discipline and Pupil-behaviour Policies – Guidance for Schools
- The Duty to Promote Disability Equality

4 Helping things get better

Avoiding discrimination

There are several positive ways of avoiding claims and complying with the duties in the EA:

- Training: senior staff need to understand their duties to children with disabilities. All staff need to be aware of the duties in the EA and to understand disability as an equality issue.
- Reviewing: a review of policies, practices and procedures should look at all the different areas of the life of the school. Make sure that you have no blanket policies that might have a negative impact on children with disabilities. This is a requirement under your equality duty.
- Finding out: information is a crucial part of meeting the EA duties. Schools need to provide opportunities for parents, and children with disabilities themselves, to share information. An important part of this will be developing parents' trust that information that they share will be handled sensitively.
- Getting further help: a range of services are available to schools. These vary from area to area, but will include area SENCOs and SENCO networks, visual impairment and hearing impairment services, equipment and toy libraries, health and social services support, voluntary organisations and parent partnership services. Charities are often a good source of information and support.
- Develop good partnerships with parents and seek their advice and support for their child.
- Always be prepared to look at your own attitudes and practices to assess whether you or your staff would benefit from more training.
- Make sure all new staff and supply staff have a good understanding of your school's policies and procedures towards SEN and pupils with disabilities.

Case study 8

A child has been identified as having a visual impairment. The playground in the school was old and uneven with potholes, so could pose a danger to the child due to their visual disability. It was requested that the school places cones in the depressions so that the child could make a distinction and avoid possible danger in the playground. Despite recommendations from the visual and mobility services and parents, the school refuses to comply and no attempt was made to put cones in the playground.

1 Was the less favourable treatment justified?
2 Was there a reasonable adjustment that could have been made?

Suggested answers can be found on page 76.

Information issues

Your school needs information about your pupil's disabilities in order to meet your duties. It is important that you seek information from parents before a child is admitted so that the necessary adjustments can be put in place in good time. However, make sure, when asking at this time, that you assure the parent that the child's disability will have no effect on their admittance.

Where it appears that a school has failed to make reasonable adjustments for a child with a disability, there are two main issues to consider from a legal point of view:

1   whether the school could have known about the child's impairment; and
2   whether an anticipatory reasonable adjustment should have been made.

Lack-of-knowledge defence

If parents choose not to tell your school that their child has a disability, you may be able to claim that you did not know about the child's disability. You would only be able to claim this if you had taken reasonable steps to find out about the child's disability.

One way to address disclosure issues is to provide separate letters with the admissions documents (see Appendix 3) asking parents if their child has any needs related to a disability that they wish to tell the school about. The form should make it clear what this information will be used for, that it will not be disclosed to anyone without the parent's consent and it will not be used to determine if the child is admitted to the school.

Your school is expected to take steps to find out if a pupil has a disability. Forming good working partnerships with parents will go a long way to encourage disclosure. It is important to help parents understand that if their child has a disability, they should work together with the school so that the child can achieve their best, but to do this requires the school to know about the child's disability.

Confidentiality

If a parent does share information about their child's disability, but asks the headteacher to keep that information confidential, this may limit what reasonable adjustments your school can make for the child, and the duties recognise this. Parents need to be aware that even if they have asked for information about their child's disability not to be passed on to any other members of staff, there could be certain instances where this may still have to be done for reasons of health and safety, emergency or public policy.

If a parent does ask you to restrict information about their child's disability, this will affect any reasonable adjustments that could be made, and your school may be able to claim that you did not know about the child's disability due to lack of knowledge, should any claims of disability discrimination occur.

Remember that it is important to document all conversations with parents regarding your school's inclusive practice towards their child. If you do not keep a record of disclosures made by parents or what has been agreed with parents, then should a claim of discrimination be brought against your school, you will have very little evidence to show all the good practices and reasonable adjustments you have made. You should keep on record any changes to the curriculum, activities or the school environment, no matter how small the reasonable adjustment may be.

Busting the myths

Myth: People with disabilities are 'not like other people' because they look, speak or behave differently.
Fact: A person's impairment is only one characteristic. We all have the same needs and rights to family life, social life, participation in society and being valued and respected.

Myth: People with disabilities are ill or infectious.
Fact: Many people live with impairment, but are healthy or active. It is not possible to 'catch' someone's impairment through contact. This fear is the result of lack of knowledge and misunderstanding.

Myth: People with disabilities can't make their own decisions because they might make a mistake.
Fact: Everyone should have the right to make decisions for themselves: even wrong ones!

Myth: You have to speak loudly to most people with disabilities, because they might have difficulty talking.
Fact: People get confused about how to communicate with a person who has a disability. They get the disabilities mixed up.

Myth: We have to talk for people with disabilities because they aren't capable.
Fact: People who take over for another person really deprive that person of a sense of self-worth and dignity.

Myth: People with disabilities don't have feelings like you – their blood is a different colour too!
Fact: People who are disabled think and feel the same as anyone, but people seem to think they should react to situations differently from other people.

Myth: People with disabilities have a poor quality of life.
Fact: This is one of the most common and damaging stereotypes, because it discourages social interactions and the development of mature relationships. People with disabilities have needs just like those who are not disabled, and they strive for as high a quality of life as other individuals. Society handicaps individuals by building inaccessible schools, theatres, homes, buses etc. The attitude that disability is a bad thing and that disability itself means a poor quality of life is often viewed as more disabling than the disability itself.

Myth: People with disabilities are inspirational, brave and courageous for living successfully with their disability.
Fact: A person with a disability is simply carrying out normal activities of living when they drive to work, go shopping, pay their bills or compete in athletic events. Access to community-based long-term service such as attendant care, access to buildings, public transportation, pavements, quality healthcare and necessary equipment enables them to carry on the same as non-disabled people.

Myth: Disability is a devastating personal tragedy.
Fact: The lives of people with disabilities are not tragic. What often disables people is the attitudes that they encounter and the environment in which they live, work and learn.

Myth: There are people with disabilities who are 'uneducable'.
Fact: People with disabilities reflect the same range of academic ability as non-disabled people, with some achieving high qualifications and undertaking high-level jobs.

Myth: Equal opportunity means that everyone is treated the same, so students with disabilities should not get any 'special treatment'.
Fact: Equal opportunity exists to provide all people with access to achieving their potential. The application of reasonable adjustments addresses barriers to access. It does not provide an advantage.

Can you think of any more?

What can we do for parents?

There is much evidence that children do better at school when their parents take an interest in their education and involve themselves in their child's homework. When considering parental involvement, we must also include the views of parents with disabilities and opinions (see the disclosure letters in Appendix 3). For example, for many parents with visual impairments, written information will not be accessible unless it is made available on tape, in large print or in braille. Written information may also be inaccessible to parents with learning disabilities.

To address the issues of hidden disabilities it would be considered a reasonable adjustment to provide ways in which parents with disabilities feel confident and comfortable disclosing their disability, or that of their child.

Clear information for parents

For parents to feel empowered, confident and encouraged to work alongside schools, they need to understand how school decisions are made that affect their child's support. If your school is open and transparent with parents it will reduce conflict and help build up an atmosphere of trust.

One way to show that your school works in an open and transparent way is to make sure your equality duty documents are easily available for parents to access so that they can see what issues you are addressing concerning SEN and disability, and any future plans the school has for improvement.

A good way to avoid conflict with parents is to provide them with regular information about how well their child has done and what more needs to be done. It would be good practice for your school to talk to the parent about what reasonable adjustments you have taken to ensure better inclusion for their child, and also to explain how much your school would value any suggestions or support from parents.

Example _____

At Chosen Hill School, Gloucestershire, in-school trained tutors (key teachers) were crucial to the success of structured conversations with parents of pupils with SEN or disabilities. Following an information evening, appointments were made by telephone and key teachers met parents after school in most instances. Any issues parents raised were met with a positive solution either on the first call or in subsequent follow-up calls.

Feedback from parents was very good, and the structured conversations have helped students develop self-esteem because parents, students and teachers are all involved in the process of learning on a regular basis.

From government green paper Support and Aspiration: A New Approach to Special Educational Needs and Disability

If a parent believes their child needs a different approach in school, it can never be assumed that they will automatically know what to do, who to ask for help or how to go about it. It is often not clear what help their child is entitled to or who provides it. Your school could play an important role in providing parents with clear information on what to do if they feel their child is not receiving the right support.

It can be very frustrating for parents trying to make sense of procedures involving getting help for their child. Your school could play a strong supporting role by just having good access to information for parents of SEN and disabled pupils. You don't have to be experts in knowing what to do for parents when they need support, but just being able to provide them with up-to-date information could make a significant difference to their relationship with the school.

Example _____

As part of the long-term development of the school, a major cultural change within the staffing structure has redefined the role of support staff and how they work with pupils and their families. Teaching assistants, learning mentors, cover supervisors and family support workers have all been replaced by a group of 20 associate teachers. Associate teachers work with students and their families and intervene and provide support in class, around school and at home.

Associate teachers have developed a close working relationship with families linking them with key support agencies and providing whatever assistance is needed to enable the family to better support their children's education.

Over the past year, collaboration between the staff, pupils and their parents has improved behaviour, and attendance has risen to 93 per cent. Persistent absence has dropped from 12.5 per cent to 3.6 per cent. At Key Stage 4, the proportion of pupils achieving at least 5 GCSEs at grades A* to C has risen from 61 per cent in 2008 to 79 per cent in 2010.

From government green paper Support and Aspiration: A New Approach to Special Educational Needs and Disability

Involving parents with disabilities can go a lot further than just providing them with information. Here are some useful points your school can think about when considering how best to improve involvement:

● Are you aware of the difficulties some parents might have in getting their children to school?

- How are elections for the governing body made fully accessible to all parents?
- Do you ensure that information, events and meetings are accessible to all parents?
- How do you promote a school ethos that values diversity, including children and adults with disabilities?
- Do you seek advice from relevant organisations about how to make your buildings accessible?
- Do staff receive disability equality training?

The responsible body

The make-up of the responsible body of a school depends on what type of school it is. It may be a group of governors, the local authority or a proprietor.

Lack of knowledge of equality law within responsible bodies is often a contributing factor when schools are taken to a tribunal. If school governors or proprietors do not understand the concept of less favourable treatment or reasonable adjustments, then mistakes are likely to be made when a parent submits a claim of discrimination. In my own tribunal case I had a preliminary meeting with the school vice chair of governors, but because of his lack of understanding about his school's duties, he would not accept that any discrimination had taken place. The subsequent tribunal case was unnecessary since it was quite evident that discrimination *had* taken place.

To this day it saddens me that the vice chair of governors chose to become defensive and hostile towards me. It was that attitude, lack of training and unwillingness to find a solution and work alongside others that caused him to advise the head wrongly and ultimately lose a tribunal case. It gave me no pleasure to win, as it was so unnecessary to have to go through this process when all that may have been needed was a discussion about what reasonable adjustments could have been made, and who the school could have worked with and consulted.

I have been a school governor myself so I know that it is a demanding role. Nevertheless, school governors have a general responsibility for the conduct of the school with a view to promoting high standards of educational achievement for all. Does your school's governing body have the right training? Would they know what to do if a parent made a claim of disability discrimination against your school?

Governor training in equality law is one of the courses provided by Inclusive Choice Consultancy (www.inclusivechoice.com).

The tribunal process

This section describes the process of an alleged act of discrimination against the school, and how it may be resolved, up to and including the SEND tribunal process. The process is shown as a flow diagram in Figure 4.1.

The process, from where it involves schools, starts when a parent of a child with a disability believes that the school has discriminated against their child because of the child's disability. The school should have internal procedures for dealing with parent's complaints, and these should be used first of all.

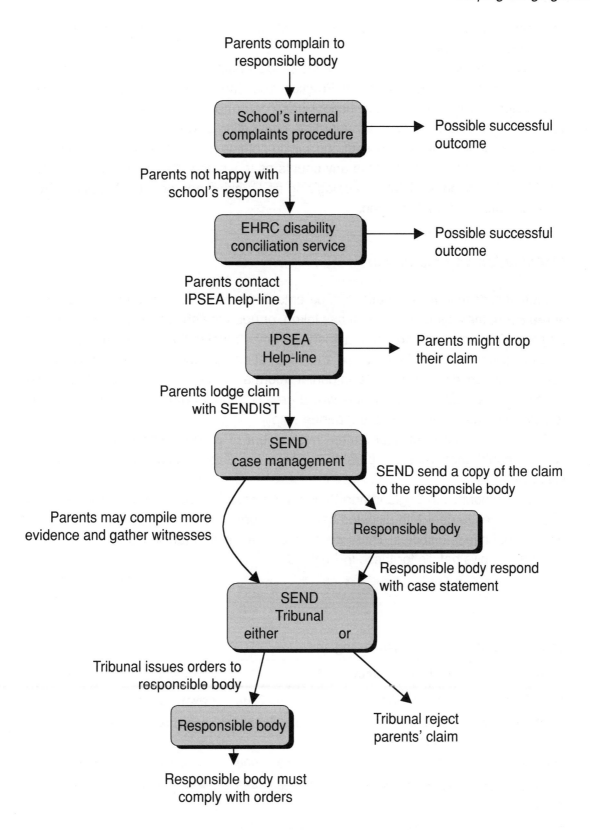

Figure 4.1 A flowchart of the tribunal process

Internal processes

It is important that the responsible body (the governing body or proprietor) is fully trained in its statutory duties towards pupils with disabilities, because it needs to know whether its school may have been discriminatory, and to make amends and plan changes at this early stage if possible.

The responsible body should review the child's treatment and, together with the information in this book, the Codes of Practice from the EHRC and any other relevant information, decide whether the school has conformed to the legislation. Defending yourself at tribunal is likely to be very time-consuming and expensive. Tribunal cases can be demoralising for school staff and will do nothing to foster good relationships with parents and pupils, so if you have any doubts as to whether the school acted correctly, admitting the school's mistakes, apologising and making appropriate changes is by far the best outcome for all involved.

Conciliation and mediation

Sometimes, despite the best efforts of parents and schools, they find they are unable to agree about the actions the school has taken, or upon the special educational provision for the child. In this situation, formal mediation may resolve the disagreement.

Many parents benefit from advice and information from their local parent partnership services, which exist to provide impartial information and advice about their child's special educational needs. Schools would greatly benefit from building strong working relationships with their local parent partnership.

If the parents are not happy after involvement of parent partnership services, the school should encourage the parents to use a conciliation service before lodging any claim with SEND.

Local authorities in England and Wales must have independent disagreement resolution services to deal with disputes between parents and schools in relation to special educational needs disputes. There are various mediation agencies around the country. Table 4.1 shows details for these in England.

Table 4.1 Mediation agencies in England.

Area	Mediation agency	Phone	Website
North East	Mediation Works	0800 953 0662	www.mediation-works.co.uk
West Midlands	Midlands SEN Mediation Service	01952 275038	www.midlandssenmediation.com
London	KIDS	020 7837 2900	www.londonsenmediation.org.uk
South East and South Central	Global Mediation	0800 064 4488	www.globalmediation.co.uk
Eastern	ConSENsus	01284 757 788	
Suffolk	Cambridge Family Mediation Service	01223 576308	www.cambridgefms.co.uk
South West	Wessex Mediation Service	0845 0529487	www.wessexmediation.co.uk
East Midlands	Together Trust	0161 283 4801	www.togethertrust.org.uk

Admissions

Admission appeal panels are independent appeal panels set up (by the admissions authority for the school) to hear appeals against admissions decisions for maintained schools and academies. They also deal with disability discrimination claims in relation to admissions decisions for maintained schools and academies.

Exclusions

Independent appeal panels consider disability discrimination in relation to all permanent exclusions from local authority maintained schools.

IPSEA

If the parents are still not happy, they may lodge a claim of discrimination with the SEND Tribunal service. Since the tribunal is a legal body, and the question of whether the school has broken the law or not can be very difficult for lay people to understand, the parents are advised to use the service provided by the Independent Parental Special Education Advice (IPSEA) for legal advice. IPSEA discourages parents from going to tribunal except as a last resort, so as a school, if you feel that you have followed the law and best practice, it would be beneficial to everyone to advise the parents to use IPSEA.

If IPSEA believes that the school is in the wrong, and the school still does not accept any wrongdoing, then IPSEA may provide legal representation for the parents at tribunal.

The Special Educational Needs and Disability Tribunal

The parents lodge a claim of discrimination against the responsible body (i.e. the school governing body) to the SEND tribunal by completing a claim form, which includes their case statement. This should describe what happened, preferably with dates, and how they think their child has been discriminated against. They must show that their child is disabled, that the alleged discrimination was connected to the child's disability, and that it was not justified. They also detail what it is they are asking the tribunal to do.

SEND then send a copy of the claim to the responsible body. The responsible body must respond to the claim with their own case statement and any evidence with which they want to reply, within 30 days of receiving the copy of the claim. This response is copied to the parents by SEND. At this point the responsible body must choose how they want to deal with the claim:

- Do they intend to dispute the claim?
- Will they seek to resolve it without the need for a hearing?
- How will they present their case at a hearing?
- What case will they make in written evidence?

The parents' claim form includes a section in which they say how they would like to see things put right. These may be things the responsible body is prepared to do without the need for a tribunal. If the responsible body agrees that there has been discrimination but plans to put things right, the parents may be prepared to withdraw their claim. It is best if disputes can be resolved by agreement between the responsible body and the parents. It is quite proper to discuss the matter while a tribunal claim is pending. Communication difficulties may well have been a factor in the dispute.

SEND arrange a date for an initial hearing within ten weeks of the submission of the parents' claim. Both the parents and the responsible body can bring up to five witnesses to the hearing. The hearing normally takes one day but can take longer. The tribunal's decision is normally received within about ten days of the final hearing.

The order in the SEND decision is binding on the responsible body. The responsible body has a duty to do what has been ordered, and normally has a limited time within which it must carry out the order. The time runs from the day after the order is sent out. The period allowed varies depending on the kind of order. The tribunal judge normally includes the time limits for carrying out the order within the written decision. SEND's role ends at this point. They have no power to supervise how and when the order is carried out.

If the responsible body does not do what has been ordered within the time limit stated in the decision, the parents can appeal directly to the Secretary of State for Education.

It is important that schools realise that whereas an appeal to SEND against a decision made regarding a pupil's *special educational needs* is an appeal against the local authority and must be defended by the local authority, appeals against *disability discrimination* is against the school's responsible body and therefore must be defended by them, not the local authority.

Additional resources

These booklets can be found on the Inclusive Choice website:

- A Guide to the Law for School Governors
- Disability Discrimination in Schools – How to Make a Claim – A Guide for Parents
- Disability Discrimination in Schools – How to Make a Claim – A Guide for Responsible Bodies
- Disabled Parents and Schools – Barriers to Parental Involvement in Children's Education
- Early Years and the Disability Discrimination Act
- Education Act 1996
- Effective Leadership – Ensuring the Progress of Pupils with SEN and Disabilities
- How Do I Make a Claim – A Guide to Taking a Part 4 Schools DDA Case
- IPSEA Annual Review 2006–2007
- Leading on Inclusion (multiple documents and PowerPoint slides)
- Maximising Progress – Ensuring the Attainment of Pupils with SEN
- SEN Code of Practice
- Supporting Disabled Parents' Involvement in their Children's Education
- A Parent's Guide to the Equality Act and their Child's Education

5 And finally...

- *The EA only applies to people with a physical or sensory impairment; true or false?*

  False. The EA does apply to people with a physical or sensory impairment but also to people with a wide range of other impairments, including learning difficulties and a range of medical conditions such as HIV and cancer.

- *Alterations to improve access only apply to the physical environment; true or false?*

  False. Physical alterations are only a small part of the changes that may be needed to allow people with disabilities to access services. Attitudes and policies of the school are more likely to restrict access.

- *Reasonable adjustments are likely to be costly; true or false?*

  False. Whilst some reasonable adjustments may be costly, most reasonable adjustments cost little or nothing. In a 2007 study of organisations' responses to the EA, the majority of those who had made adjustments found them to be easy, with 69 per cent of employers reporting no difficulties. Costs may be borne by the local authority for a statemented child, or by other organizations such as the local council's visual and hearing impaired support, or charities.

Commonly raised issues

'We didn't know he was disabled'

The definition of disability in the Equality Act is a person who has:

> a mental or physical impairment that has a long-term and substantial adverse effect on their ability to carry out normal day-to-day activities.

'Long-term' means a year or more, and 'substantial' means more than minor or trivial.

This includes many more children than is normally thought. Both terms set quite a low threshold and therefore increase the number of pupils who are covered by the definition. There may be around 750,000 children under 16 in the UK who are classed as disabled, about 7 per cent of the population.

Many pupils may not think of themselves as being disabled. Their parents may not think of them as being disabled either. That does not stop them being covered by the EA.

'The National Curriculum means I can't differentiate work'

Integral to the National Curriculum is a statutory statement: 'Inclusion: providing effective learning opportunities for all pupils'. This is usually known as the National Curriculum Inclusion Statement. It sets out three principles that are essential to the development of a more inclusive curriculum:

- setting suitable learning challenges;
- responding to pupils' diverse learning needs;
- overcoming potential barriers to learning and assessment for individuals and groups of pupils.

Rather than constraining what schools can do, the National Curriculum requires schools to adapt their approach to enable all pupils to access the curriculum.

'We can't take this child without a full-time support assistant'

A support assistant may be an important part of a pupil's special educational provision, but placing conditions on the admission of a pupil with a disability may amount to discrimination.

You mustn't make assumptions about the support a pupil will need without having made a careful assessment. You must assess all the available evidence and not make a decision based on initial concerns or impressions. If the child is transferring from another school, there should be plenty of information available from the previous school.

The effect on league tables

Many schools find that the changes they make for pupils with disabilities make the school a better place for teaching and learning. This can lead to better outcomes for all children. Many schools also focus on improving measures of pupil progress, and the value-added measures tables within published league tables reflect that.

The impact on other pupils

Again, the changes schools make for pupils with disabilities can make the school a better place for other pupils too. The best change you can make in your school to include children with disabilities is in the attitudes of the staff and other pupils. Improving that will make the school a much better place for all children.

Giving out medicines

The EA does not *require* members of staff to administer medicines. If your staff agree to administer medicines, your school should follow the Department for Education guidance, 'Managing medicines in schools and early years settings', which is available on their website.

The Code of Practice for Schools also explains schools' duties and states:

Where the administration of medicines is not in someone's contract, it is entirely acceptable for staff to volunteer to administer medicines. It may place a pupil with a disability at a substantial disadvantage if a school forbids staff to volunteer.

Exclusion to get rid of the problem

Exclusion is not a reasonable adjustment. If the exclusion is for a reason related to the pupil's disability it may be discriminatory. Many of the schools that have been most successful at including pupils will disabilities demonstrate a positive approach to managing behaviour and report low or no exclusions. A differentiated behaviour policy between certain children with disabilities and non-disabled children, that is explained to all pupils, can help reduce the number of exclusions and ensure that your school is not discriminating against pupils with disabilities with behavioural difficulties.

The Codes of Practice

The SEN Code of Practice provides advice to schools on carrying out their statutory duties to identify, assess and make provisions for children's special educational needs. Although it is still based around the Disability Discrimination Act, which preceded the Equality Act, disability law has changed very little between the two acts, and so virtually all the information in the SEN Code of Practice is still relevant now. At the time of writing this book, the EHRC had not yet produced the final version of the Code of Practice for Schools to cover the Equality Act, but one may now be available as a free download from the EHRC website.

The Code of Practice does not impose legal obligations, nor is it an authoritative statement of the law. However, it can be referred to in legal proceedings. A tribunal, appeal panel or court must take into account any part of the Code that appears to be relevant in proceedings. If schools follow the guidance in the Code, it may help to avoid an adverse judgment by a tribunal, appeal panel or court.

School improvement and the Equality Act

The key questions on the following pages were developed by Bath and North-East Somerset local authority to inform the school improvement process. The purpose was to promote discussion and sustain action, to help schools plan and make reasonable adjustments and to embed inclusive into the thinking of the whole school.

Are you a 'can do' school?

For each question, provide evidence or state how you know the answers. Also ask yourself what the impacts of your efforts are, and are they making a difference?

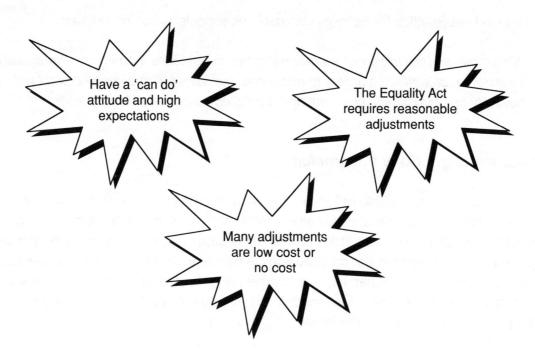

Figure 5.1 Key questions.

Additional resources

These booklets can be found on the Inclusive Choice website:

● Extending Inclusion
● Making Reasonable Adjustments for Disabled Pupils
● Managing Medicines in Schools and Early Years Settings – DoH
● Managing Medicines in Schools and Early Years Settings – Unison
● SEN Code of Practice
● Code of Practice for Schools

Table 5.1 Checklist for inclusive practice in your school.

Openers	Prompts/second order questions
Are *all* staff aware of their duties under the Equality Act?	Including: ● teachers ● learning support staff ● secretarial and administrative staff ● bursar and premises manager ● caretaker and cleaning staff ● lunch time staff including caterers ● peripatetic staff ● volunteers and helpers What does it mean for their practice? How has it made a difference?
Are all governors aware of their duties under the Equality Act?	● Have any governors attended any SEN training events? ● Which did they think most useful? ● Has there been any training for the whole governing body? ● Has 'provision for pupils with disabilities' been discussed or been an agenda item for governors? ● Does the head include a section in the head's report to governors?
Which pupils are identified as disabled?	● What is the range and distribution of pupils with disabilities? ● Do you have any means of checking that you are considering the full range of disability when identifying pupils and their needs? ● Are pupils consulted – able to express an opinion about their disability? How?
What provision is made for pupils with disabilities?	● Are pupils consulted – able to express an opinion about their provision? How? ● Were you able to anticipate the provision needed? ● What do you think you need to anticipate now?
Do pupils with disabilities have full access to every area of school life?	● Curriculum, events, activities? ● All parts of the school site? ● Off-site events and activities? ● Pupil information? ● How have you been able to achieve full access? ● What adjustments did you have to/elect to make? ● What do you need to do to achieve full access?
Is there a statement in the school's prospectus?	● Is it easy to find? ● Does it cover the three main areas? ● Is the prospectus disability friendly/inclusive (available in a range of formats)?
Is the school securing accessibility in its range of policies – curriculum and procedural?	● How do you consider access for pupils with disabilities in your policy review process? ● Which policies have you reviewed in this way so far? ● What is the priority list for the next reviews? ● What were the criteria for the priority list?

Postscript

Disability legislation is not always straightforward but your attitude to inclusion can be. Remember to perform an 'appreciative inquiry' into what is great about your school. Do you know what your school strengths in inclusion are? Are you building on these?

Is your school positive about inclusion and does it show? What role are you playing in the successful inclusion of pupils with SEN and disabilities? These are all questions that are meant to challenge you to think about what part you play in the successful inclusion of children with disabilities in your school.

We are the ones that we've been waiting for. I am asking you to believe. Not just in my ability to bring about real change ... I'm asking you to believe in yours.

Barack Obama, US President

Appendix 1: A quiz

How much do you know about the Equality Act in relation to disability?

1. **Who's affected?**
   Disability affects a large portion of the UK population across all age groups. But do you know in what proportion? Is it:

   a. one in three of the UK population?
   b. one in five?

2. **Defining disability 1**
   In one sense, a person with a disability is defined as someone who has an impairment that has a substantial and long-term effect on their ability to carry out normal day-to-day activities. Would a candidate having diabetes be defined as disabled under the EA?

   a. Yes
   b. No

3. **Defining disability 2**
   A person with a disability is also defined as someone who has a mental impairment that has a substantial and long-term effect on their ability to carry out normal day-to-day activities. Would a candidate with depression be defined as disabled under the EA?

   a. Yes
   b. No

4. **Defining disability discrimination**
   The EA defines disability discrimination as failing to make a 'reasonable adjustment' when people with disabilities are placed at a 'substantial disadvantage'. Which of these instances might be discriminatory?

   a. A school does not make special arrangements for its candidates with disabilities who are taking public exams.
   b. A school reviews its policy on bullying to ensure that it is linked to disability.

5. **Which of these is correct?**
   The EA deems that less favourable treatment has occurred when a child with disabilities is treated:

   a. less favourably than someone else;
   b. for a reason related to the child's disability;
   c. when it cannot be justified.

6. **The EA says that less favourable treatment that is justified is not unlawful discrimination. Name two ways in which less favourable treatment may be justified under the Act:**

   ● _____

   ● _____

7. **The EA requires schools and local authorities to make reasonable adjustments to ensure that pupils with disabilities are not at a substantial disadvantage. Reasonable adjustments meet the statutory requirements when they:**

   ● _____

   ● _____

   ● _____

   ● _____

8. **Name two documents that provide advice to schools on carrying out their statutory duties to identify, assess and make provisions for children's special educational needs.**

   ● _____

   ● _____

Quiz answers

1. Who's affected?

Disability affects a large portion of the UK population across all age groups. But do you know in what proportion?

b. One in five. There is a person with a disability or a person with a long-term illness living in over one in three UK households. One in four people will experience a mental health problem at some point in their lives. Nearly 35,000 young people suffer from cancer each year. Nearly 75 per cent of those with a disability leave formal education with no qualifications.

2. Defining disability 1

In one sense, a person with a disability is defined as someone who has a physical impairment that has a substantial and long-term effect on their ability to carry out normal day-to-day activities. Would a candidate having diabetes be defined as disabled under the EA?

a. Yes. While there is no fixed list of disabilities, candidates with the following physical impairments or conditions are likely to be covered:

   ● sight or hearing impairments;
   ● cancer;
   ● HIV;
   ● diabetes;
   ● mobility difficulties.

3. Defining disability 2

A person with disability is also defined as someone who has a mental impairment that has a substantial and long-term effect on their ability to carry out normal day-to-day activities. Would a candidate with depression be defined as disabled under the EA?

a. Yes. There is no fixed list of disabilities but candidates with the following mental impairments or conditions are likely to be covered:

   ● learning disabilities;
   ● obsessive compulsive disorder (OCD);
   ● depression;
   ● schizophrenia;
   ● tendency to self-harm;
   ● manic depression.

4. **Defining disability discrimination**

   The EA also defines disability discrimination as failing to make a 'reasonable adjustment' when candidates with disabilities are placed at a 'substantial disadvantage'. Which of these instances might be discriminatory?

   a. This is likely to place pupils with disabilities at a substantial disadvantage and could be unlawful under the EA. 'Reasonable adjustments' need to be anticipatory and should not be left until a pupil with a disability has arrived. Otherwise that pupil could be placed at a substantial disadvantage.

5. **The EA deems that less favourable treatment has occurred when a child with a disability is treated:**

   a. less favourably than someone else;
   b. for a reason related to the child's disability;
   c. when it cannot be justified.

   Answer: all are included in the EA.

6. **The EA says that less favourable treatment that is justified is not unlawful discrimination. There are two ways in which less favourable treatment may be justified under the Act:**

   ● if it is the result of a permitted form of selection on ability or aptitude;
   ● if there is a reason that is both material to the circumstances of the particular case and substantial; for example, if a pupil is required to make a speech to a potential donor, you may be justified in not choosing a pupil who has a severe speech impediment.

   The 'less favourable treatment' duty does not mean that pupils with disabilities have an excuse for disruptive or antisocial behaviour. There has to be a direct relationship between the reason for the less favourable treatment and the child's disability.

7. **The EA requires schools and local authorities to make reasonable adjustments to ensure that pupils with disabilities are not at a substantial disadvantage. Reasonable adjustments meet the statutory requirements when they:**

   ● act to prevent pupils with disabilities being placed at a substantial disadvantage;
   ● are aimed at all pupils with disabilities;
   ● are anticipatory;
   ● enable pupils to participate in education and associated services.

8. **Can you name two resources that provide advice to schools on carrying out their statutory duties to identify, assess and make provisions for children's special educational needs.**

   ● The SEN Code of Practice.
   ● Code of Practice for Schools.

Appendix 2: Suggested answers to case studies

Case study 1 on page 14

> A pupil with Tourette's syndrome is admitted to a school. The school wants the pupil to have all their lessons in a separate room in case they distract other children with their involuntary noises and body movements.
>
> The reasons for placing the pupil in a separate room are the involuntary noises and body movements. These are an intrinsic part of their disability.
>
> The school also claims that the inclusion of the pupil is causing significant disadvantage for the provision of efficient education for other children.

Is the less favourable treatment related to the child's disability?

The reasons for placing the child in a separate room are the involuntary noises and body movements. These are an intrinsic part of their disability, so the less favourable treatment proposed is for a reason that relates to the child's disability.

The school seeks to justify the less favourable treatment on the basis that the child might distract the other pupils. In this case the reason is based on general assumptions about the child and about the other pupils and is unlikely to constitute a material and substantial reason. This is likely to be unlawful discrimination.

The treatment that the child was to receive has to be compared with the treatment that other pupils would receive who did not make involuntary noises and body movements. This child would be isolated from the curriculum and from their peers in a way that others would not. So, for a reason that relates to their disability, this child is being treated less favourably than another child to whom that reason does not apply.

Case study 2 on page 18

> An 11-year-old girl with learning difficulties applies to go to a school that selects its intake on the basis of academic ability. She fails the entrance test. She is refused admission.

1. *Was there less favourable treatment?*

The refusal to admit the girl is based on her performance in the test. Her performance in the test is related to her learning difficulties, so this is less favourable treatment for a reason that relates to the child's disability. The treatment that she received has to be compared with the treatment that other children received who have passed the test. The treatment was less favourable as she was refused admission.

2. *If so, was the less favourable treatment justified?*

Yes.

3. *If so, why is it justified?*

The school has operated its selective criteria objectively and the less favourable treatment is likely to be justified because it is the result of a permitted form of selection. This is likely to be lawful.

Case study 3 on page 18

A school has received a number of complaints from local shopkeepers about the rowdy and disruptive behaviour of some of its pupils. It decides that the pupils in question should be banned from taking part in a school theatre visit because of their behaviour. One of the pupils has a hearing impairment.

1. *Was there less favourable treatment by the school?*

The rowdy and disruptive behaviour is not directly related to the pupil's impairment. The ban from the trip may be less favourable treatment, but it is not for a reason related to the pupil's disability.

2. *Can it be justified?*

Any less favourable treatment is not for a reason related to the pupil's disability, therefore it *can* be justified.

Case study 4 on page 22

A boy with Down's Syndrome had been attending a mainstream secondary school successfully. Following an annual review it was agreed that a teaching assistant should support the boy in some of his lessons. One of the boy's subject teachers claimed that having another adult in the classroom would be disruptive and make the child's inclusion incompatible with the efficient education of other children. The school therefore argued that it could not continue to provide mainstream education for that pupil.

1. *Was the school justified in its actions?*

Refusing the child mainstream education on these grounds would be an abuse of the efficient education provision. Where a child's statement specifies they should receive support from a teaching assistant, the assistant must be allowed into the classroom.

2. *What reasonable steps could the school have taken?*

The reasonable steps to ensure that the inclusion of a secondary-aged pupil with Down's Syndrome is not incompatible with efficient education of other children may include:

- identifying a named member of staff to oversee the social and curriculum aspects of the pupil's inclusion, and liaise with parents and outside agencies;
- planning an individualised and differentiated curriculum, by identifying links between the content of whole-class work and the learning objectives appropriate to the child's abilities;
- adjusting the balance of the curriculum to allow for additional time to be spent on such areas as expressive and receptive language, and personal, social and life skills;
- arranging for in-class support from a teaching assistant and securing appropriate training for the teaching assistant, from the local education authority or other sources;
- training subject teachers in using teaching styles that include visual prompts to support curriculum delivery, delivering instructions in short chunks, checking for understanding, and giving the pupil time to process language and respond;
- providing for alternative means of access to tasks involving reading and writing;
- ensuring access to appropriate ICT – for example, talking word-processor software;
- encouraging peer support – for example, by setting up a 'circle of friends' who have chosen to plan ways in which they can help the pupil access the curriculum and the social opportunities provided by the school;
- adhering to teaching timetables, routines and school rules explicitly, and allowing the pupil time to learn them;
- arranging for a key worker to meet regularly with the pupil to discuss positives and difficulties, build on successes and sustain meaningful links with home.

Case study 5 on page 24

A pupil with Tourette's Syndrome is stopped from going on a school visit because he has used abusive language in class. His involuntary swearing is a symptom of his Tourette's Syndrome. The school has a policy of banning pupils from trips and after-school activities if they swear or are abusive to staff. The reason for not allowing the pupil to go on the school visit is his use of abusive language.

1. *Was there less favourable treatment, and if so is it justified?*

The reason was directly related to his disability.

In this case the responsible body might argue that the inclusion of the pupil on the visit would make the maintenance of discipline impossible. This may constitute a material and substantial reason. However, the responsible body would need to have considered the extent to which the pupil's behaviour could have been managed.

2. *What document could the school have referred to in order to seek guidance so as not to discriminate?*

The SEN Code of Practice and the Code of Practice for Schools are the first documents to refer to. The child's statement (if they have one) will contain a lot of information about that child's difficulties and will allow you to plan the class's education with all pupils in mind. The Equality Act itself can always be referred to if you are in any doubt, although its language is of course rather technical.

3. *Was there a reasonable adjustment that could have been made?*

The policies and practices of the school need reviewing. Having policies that some pupils are just not *able* to comply with sets those children up to fail. Planning of visits must include the support needs of *all* the children and be anticipatory. Setting up a differentiated behaviour plan, would be appropriate in this circumstance.

4. *What if your visit was to place where the swearing could cause considerable offence, e.g. a religious institution?*

Contact the institution in advance and discuss the issue with them. If they are unwilling to accept the child and no alternative institution can be found, then redesign the lesson so that a visit is not necessary. All this should be done in advance of pupils or parents being aware that a visit was being arranged so as to prevent ill feeling towards the child with disabilities.

Note: the 'less favourable treatment' duty does not mean that pupils with disabilities have an excuse for disruptive or antisocial behaviour. There has to be a direct relationship between the reason for the less favourable treatment and the child's disability.

Case study 6 on page 48

A school is planning a skiing trip for all pupils in year 8. One of the pupils is a wheelchair user and would need support when using skis. The school informs the pupil's parents that they cannot take him because they won't have enough staff to offer support for him on the trip.

1. *Since the less favourable treatment is not on the school premises, can it be justified?*

The explanatory notes to Special Educational Needs And Disability Act 2001 state that:

> *It is intended that all teaching during school hours, other teaching, and activities such as after school clubs, school trips and school orchestras are covered by the duties.*

A school trip is an associated service provided by the school. No distinction is made in the legislation between a school trip in term time and a school trip outside of term time. It follows, then, that the Equality Act applies equally to both.

2. *Since the trip is outside of school hours, do the teachers still need to follow the EA as they are then 'private citizens'?*

   The Act covers school trips and, therefore, it appears irrelevant when the school trip takes place. A teacher may volunteer their time but they are clearly acting in their capacity as a member of staff for the school.

3. *If the school is a selective school, can they select pupils for the skiing trip based on aptitude, since there are a limited number of places available?*

   A limited number of places would affect all children at the school, not just any children with disabilities, and so is not discrimination in itself. Different forms of selection are permitted in different schools. For example, specialist schools can give priority in their admissions criteria to a proportion of pupils who show a particular aptitude for the subject in which the school specialises. However, these permitted criteria are concerned with school admissions, *not* school trips.

4. *Could the school claim that the skiing trip is not part of the curriculum, and therefore missing it would not be detrimental to the pupil's education?*

   A refusal to take a child would need to be justified with regard to less favourable treatment, reasonable adjustments and the material and substantial factors. It appears possible that the loss of opportunity to go on a ski trip would not be found to diminish a child's progress, to the extent that it would put the child at a substantial disadvantage when compared with their peers. As such, less favourable treatment may well be justified within the meaning of the Act. This would be dependent on the particular circumstances of a case.

5. *If the facilities at the resort are not suitable for a disabled child, would the school still be in breach of the EA?*

   The school is under a duty to make reasonable adjustments and these must be anticipatory. For less favourable treatment to be justified, material and substantial factors of a particular case would need to be looked at. If the resort chosen by the school *did* fail to provide facilities for children with disabilities this may well be found to be a breach of duty to provide reasonable adjustments. The failure by a school to make reasonable adjustments would be dependent on a child's particular individual circumstances.

Case study 7 on page 49

> A pupil with cerebral palsy who uses a wheelchair is on a trip with her class to an outdoor activity centre. The teachers arrange to take the class on a 12-mile hike over difficult terrain but, having carried out a risk assessment, they decide that the pupil who uses a wheelchair will be unable to accompany her class, for health and safety reasons.

1. *Is the less favourable treatment for a reason that is related to the pupil's disability?*

    This is less favourable treatment for a reason that relates to the pupil's cerebral palsy, namely the use of a wheelchair.

2. *Is it justified?*

    The responsible body is likely to be able to justify the less favourable treatment for a material and substantial reason: a risk assessment, carried out in relation to this particular pupil in the particular setting in which she would have to travel indicated that the health and safety of the pupil and her classmates could be jeopardised if she were to attempt the hike. This is likely to be lawful.

    An inclusive approach towards this trip would have been to perform an anticipatory risk assessment before the trip, and arrange with the outdoor activity centre to involve the pupil in another activity running in parallel with the hike that did meet health and safety requirements. The school should make sure where possible that the pupil with cerebral palsy is included on all activities with their peers.

    Health and safety is an important issue when planning school trips, but it should not be used as a blanket assumption that if a risk has been identified, the school need do no more to include the child because of the identified risk.

Case study 8 on page 51

A child has been identified as having a visual impairment. The playground in the school was old and uneven with potholes so could pose a danger to the child due to their visual disability. It was requested that the school place cones in the depressions so that the child could make a distinction and avoid possible danger in the playground. Despite recommendations from the visual and mobility services and parents, the school refuses to comply, and no attempt was made to put cones in the playground.

1. *Was the less favourable treatment justified?*

    No, the less favourable treatment is not justified. Having been given advice, there was no reason why they were not set out.

2. *Was there a reasonable adjustment that could have been made?*

    Yes, the cones could have been placed in the depressions in the playground much earlier.

The SEND tribunal finding was as follows:

The need to have cones was identified some time before the child arrived at the school. In the end the visiting TA was required to sort out the matter. Had the school SENCO been involved, that person could have made suitable arrangements. The school had advice from the visual impaired teacher, TA and LEA mobility officer. The cones were required because of the child's visual impairment. The failure to place those cones in the playground meant that the child was treated less favourably as a result of his disability.

Appendix 3: Disclosure letters

Dear Parent,

Your support for your child's education is crucial to their progress. If your child has a disability, it is even more important that we work together so they can achieve their best, but to do this requires the school to know about the child's disability.

The school has a duty under the Equality Act to make 'reasonable adjustments' for children with disabilities. In order to make these adjustments, some information regarding your child's disability may have to be disclosed to certain members of staff in the school.

Detailed information about the nature of your child's impairments or medical information will not be passed on unless it is relevant to making reasonable adjustments. You can request that no information is passed on to others, or you can request that information is restricted to certain people. However, you should be aware that if you do this it could limit the types of adjustments the school can make for your child.

I consent to data regarding my child's disability to be passed on (please tick):

Yes ☐   No ☐   Restricted ☐

If you have ticked 'Restricted', please list below who you consent to information being passed to, or you may like to discuss this further with the school.

Pupil's name   _____

Parent's signature   _____

Date   _____

You should be aware that even if you have asked for information about your disability not to be passed on to any other members of staff, there could be certain instances where this may still have to be done for reasons of health and safety, emergency or public policy. Information about disability is classed as sensitive personal data and will be processed by the school in accordance with the Data Protection Act 1998 and the school's data protection policy.

Dear Parent/Carer

As you may be aware, all schools are now under a duty to:

- eliminate discrimination, harassment and victimisation;
- advance equality of opportunity between people with disabilities and non-disabled people;
- foster good relations between people with disabilities and non-disabled people.

To help achieve these aims, all schools must produce and publish information on how the school is doing in relation to disability equality. In addition, information must include a statement about the way in which people with disabilities have been involved in the development of the schools equality duty. We are therefore asking all people who make use of our school building, and who consider themselves to be disabled, to help us by completing this questionnaire. This would also include people who cannot at the current time make use of the building but would like to do so in the future.

If you could spare the time to do this, we would be very grateful.

1. How would you describe your impairment?

2. Are there any ways in which you currently find it difficult to make full use of our school facilities (for example to come into the school or to read information)?

3. Are there any ways in which the school could help you to make full use of our school facilities (for example, to come into the school or to read information)?

4 Are there any other ideas you have about ways in which the school could carry out any of the duties in the letter above?

5. Are there any other ways in which you think the school should involve people with disabilities in the creation of our Disability Equality Scheme?

Name (optional): _____

Note: the school will have to consider what other formats these letters might have to be produced in (e.g. audio tape, braille, etc.).

Index

admissions 37, 59
appreciative inquiry 1
association: discrimination by 28
attitudes 14, 30, 51

Code of Practice 7, 19, 63
communication 9
conciliation 58
confidentiality 52

DDA *see* Disability Discrimination Act
definition 6
direct discrimination 14
Disability Discrimination Act 2, 3, 12, 32, 63
disability discrimination duties 12
Disability Equality Duty, the 20, 32
disability legislation: history 2
disclosure 7, 52, 78
discrimination arising from disability 15

EHRC *see* Equality and Human Rights Commission
eligible children 41
Equality Act 3, 12
Equality and Human Rights Commission 3, 36, 63
equality objectives 36
escorts 42
exclusions 39, 59

general duty 33

harassment 28, 30, 33
hearing impairments 10, 18, 69
hidden impairments 7

indirect discrimination 15, 28, 38
information 52
insurance 46
IPSEA 59

jargon 1
justification 15, 16, 18, 46, 47
lack of knowledge 52
language 7, 9

letters 78

mediation 58
medical model 3
medicines 45, 62
misconceptions 61

parents 7, 18, 20, 21, 34, 36, 40, 42, 43, 45, 52, 54, 78
perception: discrimination by 28
permitted forms of selection 18
positive action 26
proportionate action 27

reasonable adjustments 19-26
relevance 35
responsible body 56

school improvement 63
SEND *see* tribunal
six elements 33
social model 5
Special Educational Needs: definition 6
specific duty 34
speech impairments 11

three aims 33
transport 40
tribunal 17, 39, 56
trips 46–49

victimisation 29